STATE OF RURAL AND AGRARIAN INDIA REPORT 2020

Rethinking Productivity and Populism through Alternative Approaches

RICHA KUMAR, NIKHIT KUMAR AGRAWAL,
P.S. VIJAYSHANKAR, A.R. VASAVI

INDIA · SINGAPORE · MALAYSIA

Notion Press

No. 8, 3rd Cross Street,
CIT Colony, Mylapore,
Chennai, Tamil Nadu – 600 004

First Published by Notion Press 2021
Copyright © Richa Kumar, Nikhit Kumar Agrawal,
P.S. Vijayshankar, A.R. Vasavi 2021
All Rights Reserved.

ISBN 978-1-63832-648-9

Graphics and Design by Kanikka Sersia

This report is an attempt to provide a comprehensive and critical overview of the state of contemporary rural India. It focuses on the key structural factors, especially policies and trends, that have marked rural India's economic and ecological conditions. Through this report we wish to share alternative ideas, paradigms and methodologies to address these entrenched problems and challenges. We hope the range of stakeholders—farmers, rural citizens, elected representatives, gram panchayat members, policy-makers, academics, students and interested members of the public, including farmer organisations and civil society networks, will engage with the ideas and suggestions. There is an urgent need to address the extant erasure of rural livelihoods, depletion of natural resources and the pauperization of rural citizens, which misplaced policies and outdated ideas continue to perpetuate. The key questions and the following responses in this report seek to provide some pathways towards new alternatives.

The Network of Rural and Agrarian Studies (NRAS - www. ruralagrarianstudies.org) is an all-India network of scholars, researchers, practitioners, farmers, students, and activists studying or working on issues concerning rural and agrarian India. This multidisciplinary collective has sought to promote research, support pedagogy and engage with policymaking on rural and agrarian issues since 2010.

NRAS encourages the use, reproduction, and dissemination of material in this report. Material in this report may be copied, downloaded, and printed for private study, research, and teaching purposes, or for use in non-commercial products or services, provided that appropriate acknowledgement of NRAS as the source is given and that NRAS's endorsement of users' views, products, or services is not implied in any way.

Contents

Acknowledgements

Inputs and suggestions on this report were provided by other NRAS Core Group Members: **C. Shambu Prasad, Rajeswari S. Raina, M. Vijayabaskar, Aniket Aga, Siddharth Joshi**, and **Shalini Bhutani**. We thank them for their efforts. Any omissions or errors remain our responsibility alone.

We also thank all the participants at the various annual NRAS conferences, and especially those who attended the first and second policy conference at the Indian Institute of Advanced Study, Shimla (2016) and the Indian Institute of Technology Delhi (2019).

We gratefully acknowledge the support of several institutions that have hosted the NRAS meets over the years: National Institute of Advanced Studies, Bengaluru (2010); Annamalai University, Chidambaram (2012); Indian Institute of Forest Management, Bhopal (2014); Govind Ballabh Pant Social Science Institute, Allahabad (2015); Indian Institute of Advanced Study, Shimla (2016); Nabakrushna Choudhury Centre for Development Studies, Bhubaneswar (2017); Central University of Gujarat, Gandhinagar (2018); Department of Humanities and Social Sciences, Indian Institute of Technology Delhi (2019).

NRAS activities from 2010-2020 have been funded by the following organisations: Indian Council for Social Science Research (ICSSR); ICSSR Northern Regional Council, ICSSR Eastern Regional Council, QIP/CEP Program of IIT Delhi, Department of Humanities and Social Sciences, IIT Delhi, NCDS Bhubaneswar,

Central University of Gujarat, Gandhinagar, NABARD, Mumbai, Foundation for Ecological Security (FES), Gujarat, IIAS Shimla, and Ford Foundation, New Delhi. We convey our sincere gratitude to them for their support.

We thank the World Resources Institute for providing four maps and Seema Bathla and P.K. Joshi for providing two graphs that have been included in this report. Some graphs have been sourced from government documents such as the Dalwai Committee Report and NSSO Reports. Sources for all graphs have been provided in the footnotes at the end of the report. We also thank Dwiji Guru, Sudha Nagavarapu, M. Vijayabaskar, Richa Kumar, Nikhit Kumar Agrawal, and M. N. Dinesh Kumar for providing us with photographs for use in the report. We acknowledge all these sources with gratitude.

01   Introduction

Concerns over the state of rural India have grown to become a litmus test for the nation's policies and political strategies. Even before COVID-19, the rural economy was facing severe distress. The heart-rending sight of migrant workers walking back home after the COVID-19 outbreak and the national lockdown, has opened up the nation's conscience to the vast humanitarian crisis. There is a real need for a substantive engagement with rural India. Yet, the diversity of voices and views indicate no clarity on future directions. Building upon ten years of engagement with rural and agrarian India, the NRAS Collective is bringing out this report which has two parts.

In the first part, we outline the current dominant policies and paradigms and their implications for rural residents, livelihoods, ecologies and geographies. In the second part, we present alternative ideas, methodologies, and approaches to facilitate the implementation of policies which are socially just, economically stable, ecologically sustainable and politically democratic for rural India.

The 1960s marked a significant shift in India's agricultural strategy towards a high productivity regime with its exclusive focus on

a few crops in the irrigated tracts of the country. Though this has resulted in an acceleration of agricultural growth and higher food production, monocultures of these crops have meant loss of agro-ecological diversity and practices associated with each diverse agrarian region. Crops like millets and pulses have been the least favoured, and dryland regions have received little attention. This model of high input industrial agriculture has become the established way of doing agriculture in India. This inherently fragile and high risk model has placed the natural resource base of rural India (land, water and forests) under severe stress. The long term growth path of agriculture is proving to be ecologically unsustainable and socially unjust. Compounding this is the impact of cataclysmic climate change.

These developments in agriculture, which have been reinforced in the past few years by changes in the non-farm sector of the rural economy, have given rise to unprecedented rural distress. It is now known that the non-farm sector is increasingly gaining importance at the

household level in rural India, as employment in agriculture is stagnant or declining. Non-farm employment growth has been slow in India in recent years.

Rural distress has several other manifestations like rising numbers of suicides, pervasive under-nutrition among women and children, growing disease burden and rising healthcare costs. The flows of finance, people, resources, technologies and waste are reshaping the rural-

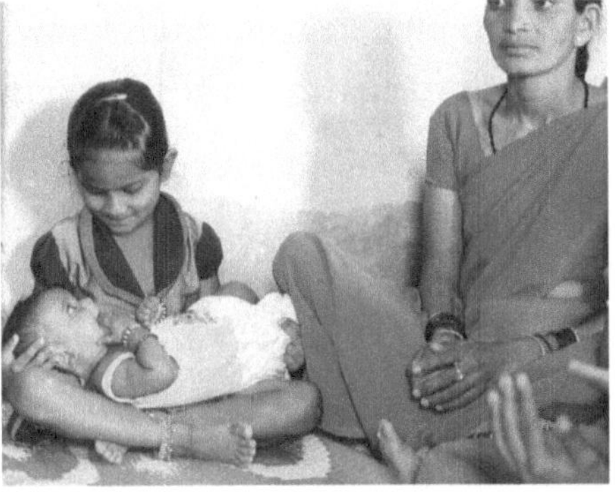

urban relationship with serious implications for ecology, health and society.

Rural India is in urgent need of an alternative vision for its sustainability and the well-being of the majority of its people. It is necessary to understand that the rural economy is an integral part of a larger ecosystem. This means reshaping our patterns of production and consumption through an understanding of the framework of co-existence or interdependence.

The economy of rural and agrarian India has been based on extractive relationships with the environment and natural resources (food, fiber, minerals, forest wealth) and policy makers, scientists and industrialists committed to modern industrial agriculture have refused to acknowledge the true value of these resources. The environment has also been converted into a sink to which waste is dumped. We must structurally address this issue and transform these relationships from extraction to co-existence, centred on the perspective of agro-ecology and combine insights from knowledge systems and practices of local communities with insights from the sciences.

This would also require us to challenge the conventional divides between urban and rural, between industry and agriculture and between farm and non-farm. Work has to be ecologically suitable, meaningful and satisfying. Given the crisis of livelihoods we face currently, the problem of the rural cannot be solved by making the rural itself redundant. There is the pressing need to develop technologies and market

relationships that can support the work of people in diverse rural livelihoods without replacing them entirely.

Articulating new legal regimes that can safeguard the needs of the marginalised majority to conserve and use natural resources must form the bedrock of new policies. But this would require concerted action and building strong alliances of people- -farmers, rural communities, urban communities, civil society actors along with the community of committed scientists, people's representatives and policymakers. Bringing the voices and experiences of the marginalised majority (the landless, tenant farmers, women farmers, forest-dwellers, fisherfolk, dalits, adivasis, rural artisans, pastoralist groups, among others) into the policy making process would strengthen the foundations of rural India's pluralism and revitalise its grassroots democratic polity.

Lastly, translating this alternative vision into practice would require abandoning conventional indicators and building new ones. We need to stop valuing growth as measured by the GDP (Gross Domestic Product). The new set of measurements take into account ecological sustainability as one of the key indicators of "green" growth. Can we recognise and value farmers for the ecosystem services that they provide, for the agro-biodiversity that they can help conserve, for the healthy food that they can grow? These alternative metrics will help us assess the ecological and social impacts of our activities, understand the positive and negative feedback loops and take informed decisions.

02

Mainstream Approaches That Have Shaped Rural and Agrarian India

I. Most Policies Tended to Have An Extractive Approach with Emphasis on Increasing Agricultural Productivity and Are

- Based on the thinking that natural resources are *infinitely available for continuous extraction* for economic growth.

- Replacing diverse, regionally viable agricultural systems and practices with *monocultures of selected crops*, sacrificing traditional cultivation methods, seed and food diversity, and nutrition.

- Promoting the *Green Revolution model* across the nation with its emphasis on industrially produced chemical inputs, hybrid seeds, and high technology, leading to chemicalisation of the environment and adverse health effects.

- Facilitated by *active state support* through subsidies on inputs (seeds, fertilisers), public investment in irrigation infrastructure, rural electrification, agricultural markets and agricultural extension, guaranteed purchase at

MSP (Minimum Support Prices) and public distribution of food, provision of cheap agricultural credit through formal institutions, and investment in agricultural research.

- Based on a paradigm of betting on the strong with a focus on a few crops and regions; led to neglect of rainfed, mountainous, forest and coastal areas and crops like millets, pulses and oilseeds. Led to *growth of regional and social inequality.*

II. The Response of the State to the Crisis of the Green Revolution Has Been to Push Populist Policies Which Include

- Continued (although fewer) subsidies that have led to a growing subsidy burden along with increased ecological damage.
- Ad-hoc, piecemeal and short term measures directed at individual cultivators such as loan waivers, insurance, price support (MSP) and income support have shifted resources away from public or community based investment in agriculture.

III. Industrialisation, Urbanisation and Modernisation have been the Key Pillars of the Mainstream Approaches to Development

- Policies are based on upholding the idea that *the transition from rural-agrarian economies to urban-industrial economies is inevitable.* The standard perspective is that a large proportion of people must be moved from rural to urban regions as part of this structural transformation of the economy. Yet, there has been *no significant job creation* in the urban economy or the rural non-farm economy.

- *Adverse integration* into the national and transnational capitalist economy (on terms and conditions of consumers or agribusiness): rural India subsidises the urban and industrial sector by transferring substantial amounts of energy and resources to it, and receiving its waste.

- Tribal regions are seen as sources of raw materials and *tribal lifestyles seen as backward,* despite their sustainability and inclusivity.

- ***Destruction of rural cottage industries*** and artisanal work by technology driven mass consumption trends and declining availability of natural resources, which creates a pool of cheap, surplus labour for urban centres.

- Corporatisation of agriculture along with institutionalising intellectual property rights that are tilted towards being vested with agri-business and not with rural citizens' innovations.

- Land is considered more valuable as a financial asset (real estate) and the financialisation of agricultural commodities has facilitated corporate involvement in agriculture. This has ***negatively affected common property resources*** (water bodies, grasslands, forests), many of which have been privatised and converted to agricultural land or into urban colonies.

- Policies are made ***without consulting farmers*** or rural citizens.

2.1 Impact of Mainstream Approaches on Natural Resource Base of Agriculture

I. Land Degradation

The extent of degraded land in India is 12 crore hectares or about 38% of our total geographical area. [50]

There is an increasing trend of farmland getting diverted for urbanisation and industries. [87][97]

India, Types of Land Degradation, NAAS 2010

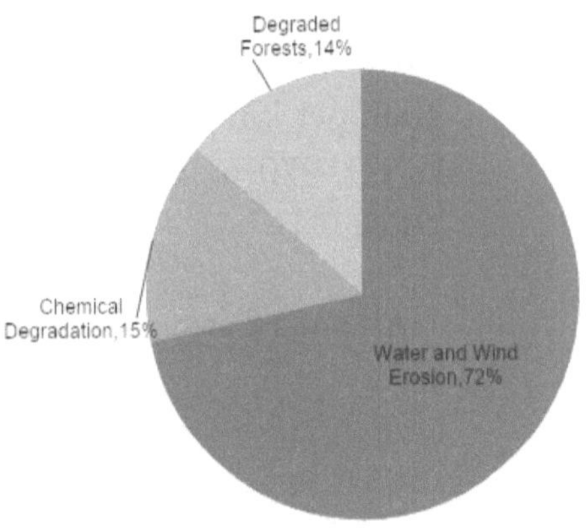

Source: [50]

State-wise Distribution of Degraded Land, 2010

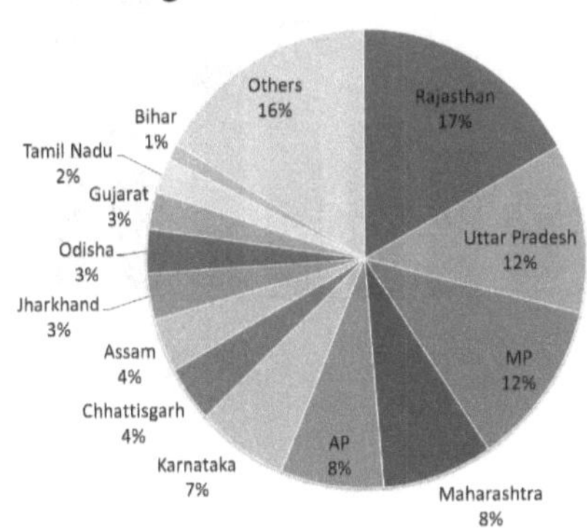

Source: [50]

The net sown area in India was 14.3 crore hectares in 1990-91 which decreased by almost 30 lakh hectares in 2014-15, which is half the size of the National Capital Region. During the same period, area under non-agricultural uses increased by almost 50 lakh hectares. [98]

II. Loss of Soil Health

- Green Revolution policies have disregarded the importance of the physical structure, (M)icrobial activity, and organic (M)atter of soil, all of which affect its (M)oisture holding capacity. [62]
- These three M's are negatively affected by chemical overuse, and especially by government policies which promote a skewed chemical fertiliser subsidy. [6]

  - This has led to a distorted Nitrogen-Phosphorus-Potassium (NPK) ratio in states such as Punjab (61.7:19.2:1), Haryana (61.4:18.7:1.), Rajasthan and Uttar Pradesh as measured in 2013. [7]
  - This has negatively impacted productivity of crops: yield of grain per kilogram use of NPK fertilizer declined from 13.4 kg in 1970 to 3.7 kg grain per hectare in irrigated areas by 2005. [7]

All India Consumption of fertilizers in '0000 tonnes

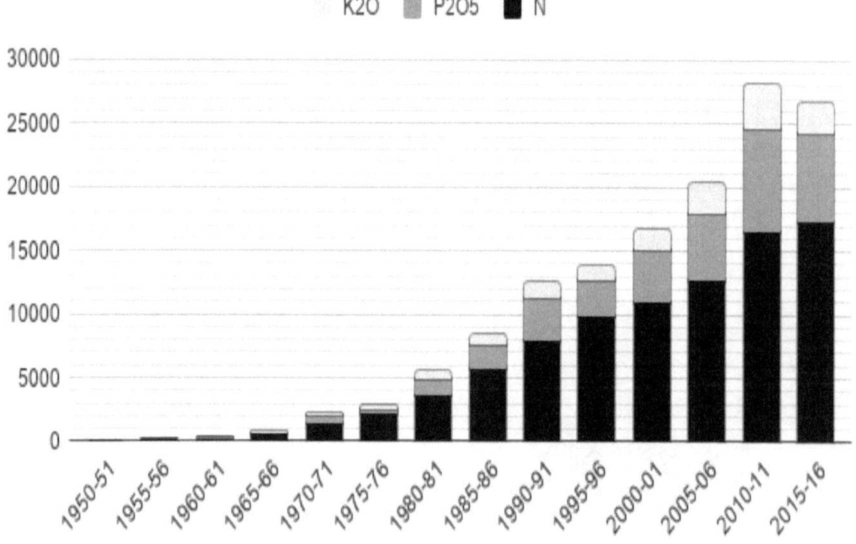

Source: [104]

Fertiliser Response Ratio in Irrigated Areas

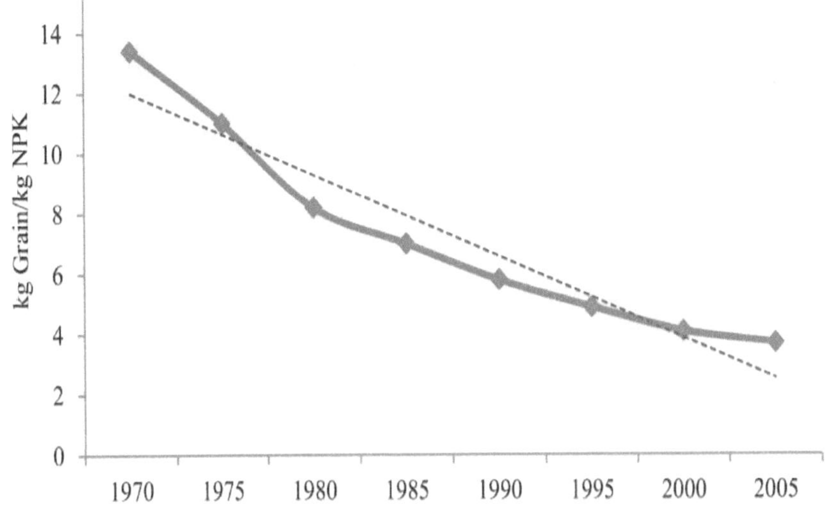

Source: [6]

- Data from the National Soil Health Card Scheme shows that of the 2.30 crore soil samples tested between 2017 and 2019, 80% reported moderate to severe deficiency in Nitrogen, 63% were found deficient in Organic Carbon and 48% were found deficient in Phosphorus. [115]
- Deficiency of minerals and micronutrients in soils has also reduced the nutritional value of the foods produced. [16]

III. Loss of Seed Varieties and Biodiversity

- More than 70,000 varieties of rice have been found on the Indian subcontinent, most of which disappeared from cultivation after the 1970s due to the Green Revolution. Now only 7000 local varieties exist, out of which only a handful are cultivated. [20][102][117]
- In the last five decades, area under millets has also been replaced by wheat, paddy, and other commercial crops. [96] Total area under millets declined from 4.5 crore hectares in 1960 to 2.9 crore hectares in 2008. [20]

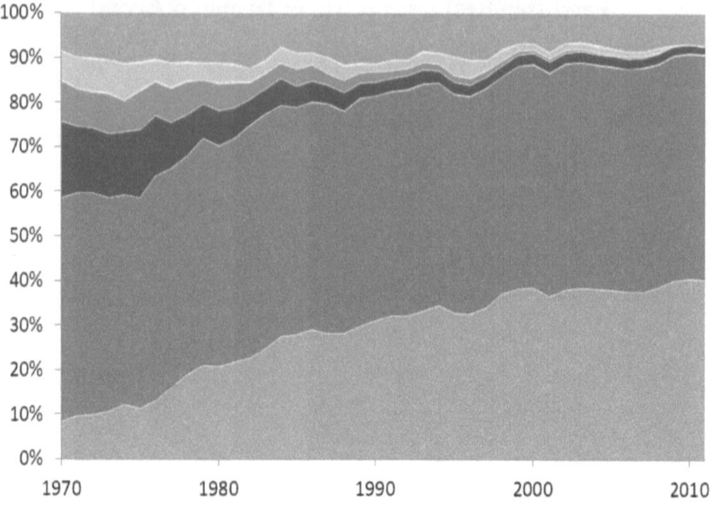

Cropping Pattern of Punjab, 1970-2010

Source: [69] **The shift towards rice and wheat cultivation in Punjab can be observed by the broadening of the red and green bands in the graph above with the narrowing of all other colour-bands between 1970-71 and 2010-11.**

- Between 1970 and 2010, area under rice and wheat together increased from 47.2% of the total cropped area to 80.3% in Punjab, while area under all other crops except cotton declined sharply [see graph above].
- While Punjab was primarily a wheat growing region, rice cultivation increased after the mid 1970s to occupy 97% of kharif sown area.

IV. Pest Attacks and Crop Losses

- Declining biodiversity has resulted in increasing frequency and virulence of pest attacks. There has been an increase of 500% in pest incidences in case of rice at an all-India level from 1965 to 2009. The number of rice pests, in the corresponding period, increased from five to fifteen. [60]

- With intensification of agriculture in the post-Green Revolution era (early 2000s) as compared to the pre-Green Revolution era (early 1960s), crop losses due to insect pests have seen an increasing trend. For cotton, which was modified from short staple diploid varieties to long staple tetra and hexaploid varieties, this increased three fold from one-fifth (18%) to one-half (50%). In maize, crop losses grew from 5% to 20%, a four-fold increase and the combined figures for sorghum and millets is a ten-fold increase from a meagre 3% to 30%. [59][116]

- With the advent of Bt cotton to control bollworm, secondary pests posed major challenges. The 2015 whitefly epidemic in the cotton belt of Punjab destroyed around 75% of the cotton crop. All the varieties of the native Indian short staple cotton species (Gossypium arboreum) were unaffected, but genetically modified (Bt) species had been bred into varieties that were known to be susceptible to this pest. [61]

- There is a ***threat of total collapse of ecosystems*** with pollinators and insects disappearing due to the use of agrochemicals. The threat to farm incomes is evident from the massive volume of pesticide use, increasing incidence of secondary pests, sale of spurious pesticides and resulting crop loss, which drive farmers into debt.

V. Over-Extraction of Groundwater

- An assessment by NASA showed that from 2002 to 2008, three states (Punjab, Haryana and Rajasthan) together lost about 109 km^3 of water leading to a decline in the water table to the extent of 0.33 metres per annum. [106] For North India as a whole it was 54 cubic kms per annum during the same period. [105]

- A recent OECD study on global water risk hotspots has identified India's north-western region as one of the top three water risk hotspots in agricultural production. [10]

- Out of 6881 groundwater units assessed in India, 1186 were over-exploited, 313 were critical, 972 were semi-critical and 100 were saline-affected. [109]

54%

of India's
Ground-
water
Wells Are
Decreasing

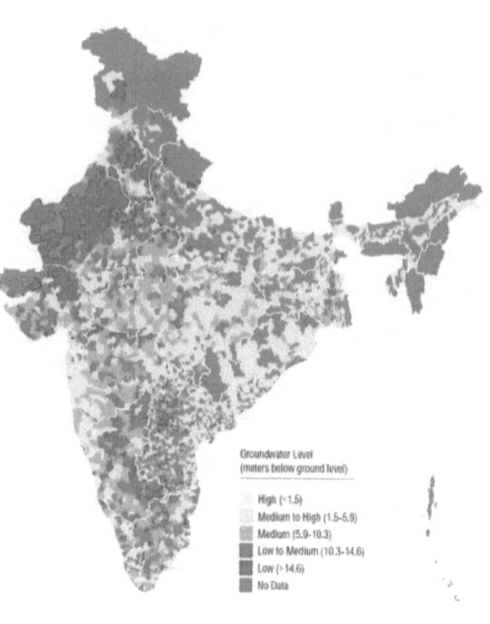

More than

100

MILLION

People Live
in Areas of
Poor Water
Quality

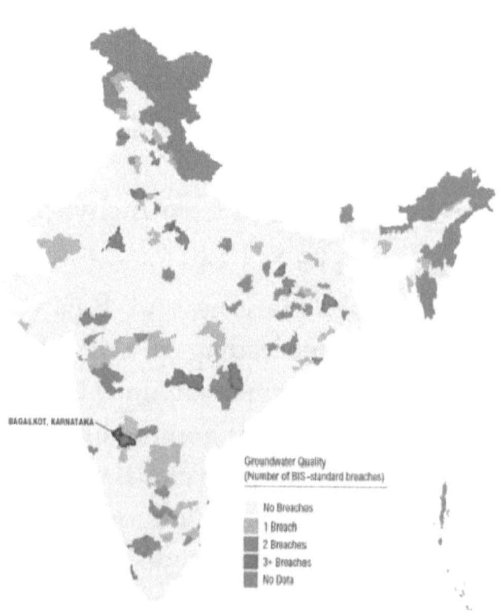

Categorisation of Blocks based on Groundwater Quality

October 12, 2020
1:18,489,298
Latest India Map
Block Categorization
SAFE
SEMI CRITICAL
CRITICAL
OVER EXPLOITED
SALINE
NO DATA

54%
of India
Faces
High to
Extremely
High
Water Stress
Baseline Water Stress
(withdrawals/available supply)
Low (<10%)
Low to Medium (10-20%)
Medium to High (20-40%)
High (40-80%)
Extremely High (>80%)
Arid & Low Water Use

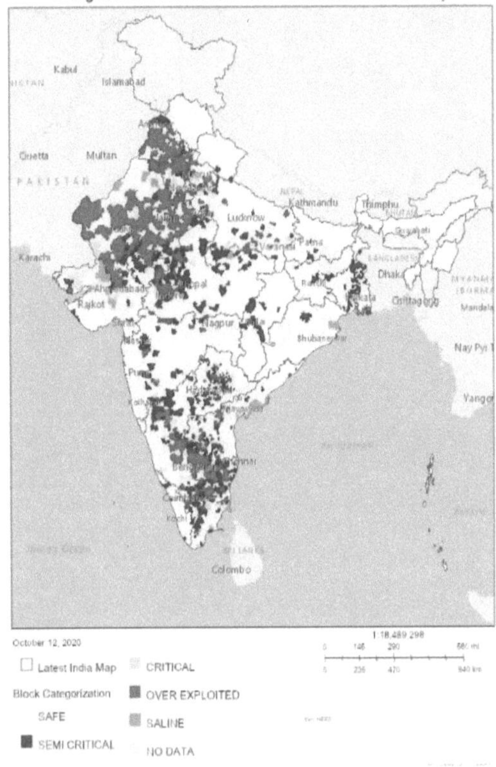

Source: [4][5]

2.2 Impact of Mainstream Approaches on Diverse Ecologies of Rural India

- Water bodies, grasslands, forests have been converted into concrete, urban zones (for housing, industry, transport, SEZs) causing lack of water recharge and *floods due to damaged drainage systems* (which is a huge problem in India's monsoon based ecology).

- Forest, river and mountain ecosystems *degraded due to mining* and building of dams (sand mining of river beds, mining for coal, bauxite and other minerals).

- *Over-extraction* of water and energy by industries, overfishing in oceans and over-extraction of forest products.

- *Toxicity of land, pollution of fresh water bodies and oceans* due to dumping of industrial and urban solid (especially plastic, biomedical and electronic waste) and liquid waste, as well as agricultural run-off.

- The Central Pollution Control Board's recent report on the quality of water in 521 rivers shows that 351 polluted river stretches on 323 rivers had Biochemical Oxygen Demand (BOD) in excess of 3 mg/l, which is the desired water quality level. 102 river stretches in 22 states were severely polluted, with the BOD concentration exceeding 6 mg/l throughout the year. [110]

Gains & Loss of Forest Area in Square Kms			
Forest Land Lost	2003-15	2015-19	Total
Very dense forest to Non-forest	545	575	1120
Mid-dense forest to Non-forest	8968	7977	16945
Total forest lost	9513	8552	18065
Forest Land Gained			
Non-forest to Very dense forest	200	233	433
Non-forest to Mid-dense forest	4569	5225	9794
Total forest gained	4769	5458	10227

Source: [89]

- *Deforestation* and *conversion of commons* into agricultural land or commercial tree plantations. According to the biennial State of Forest Report 2019, India saw the total destruction of 2145 sq km of dense forest (1.5 times the size of Delhi) in the previous two years while some gains have been made in other categories (see table above). [88]
- Burning of agricultural residues is leading to degraded soils and *air pollution.*

2.3 Looming Climate Change and Its Implications for Rural and Agrarian India

Decadal Change in Average Temperature in India in Degree Celsius

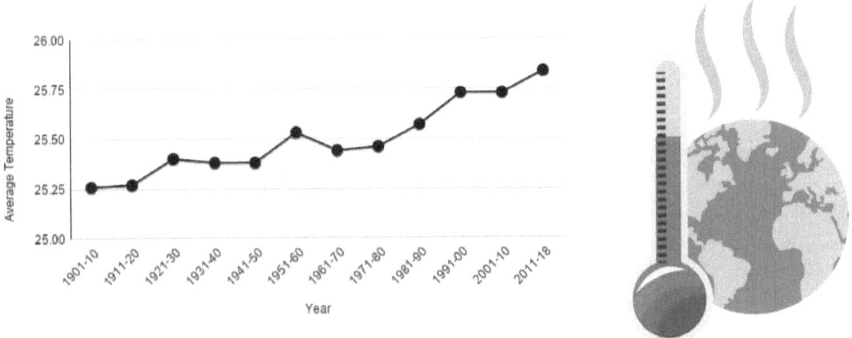

Source: [19]

There is clear evidence that *the world has already warmed by 1°C* above temperatures prior to the pre-industrial period and is likely to cross 1.5-2°C. [19]

India's average temperature has risen by around 0.7°C during 1901-2018. This rise in temperature is largely on account of GHG-induced warming, partially offset by forcing due to anthropogenic aerosols and changes in land use and land cover. [114]

Change in average rainfall between the last decade and 1950-1980 period

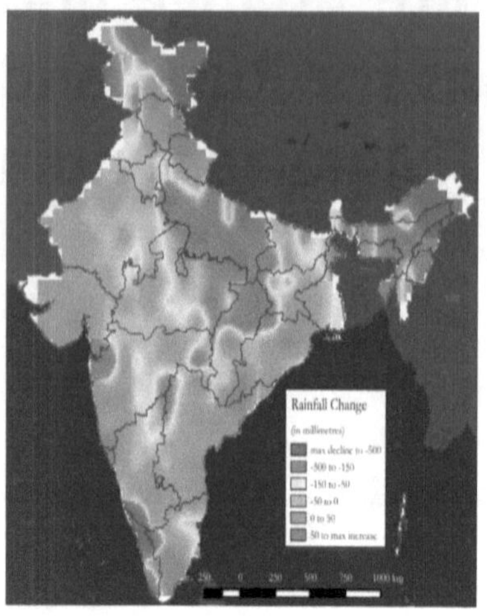

Source: [18][71]

Decreasing Rainfall and Increasing Rainfall Intensity

High-intensity rainfall events have increased, but there has also been a fall in the annual number of days with rainfall in India from around 80 days per year in early 2000s to 65 days in the past 10 years. [18] This is devastating for agriculture.

Percentage decrease in farmer's income for Kharif Crops

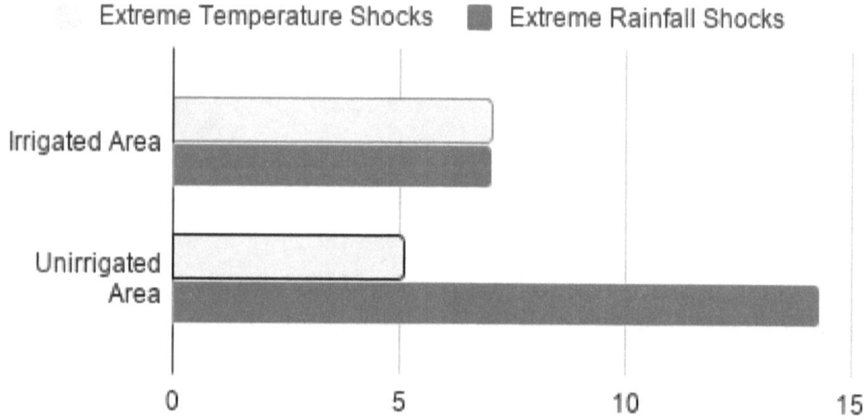

Source: [19]

Percentage decrease in farmer's income for Rabi Crops

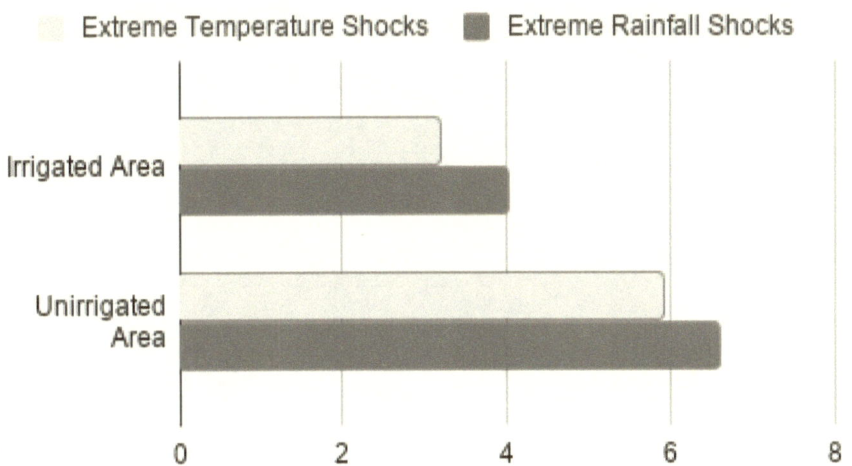

Source: [19]

- ***Extreme Climatic Events*** such as severe droughts and floods and the shifting of agricultural seasons have been observed in different agro-ecological zones of India.
- Long ***drought spells*** during kharif and increased temperatures and unseasonal heavy rains during the rabi season have caused serious distress to the farming communities in different states in recent years. [15]
- ***Sea surface temperature (SST)*** of the tropical Indian Ocean has risen by 1°C on average during 1951–2015, markedly higher than the global average SST warming of 0.7°C, over the same period. Ocean heat content in the upper 700 m (OHC700) of the tropical Indian Ocean has also exhibited an increasing trend over the past six decades (1955–2015). This will have consequences for the monsoon cycle. [114]

What is the State of Agriculturists in India Today?

I. From Cultivators to Workers to Migrants

From 1951 to 2011, the population dependent on agriculture for a livelihood has come down from more than 70% to 48%. However, in absolute terms, the number of families and the number of holdings have only increased. As of 2013, 9.02 crore (57.8%) out of an estimated 15.61 crore of rural households were agricultural households. [111]

The number of agricultural workers (cultivators + agricultural labourers) increased steadily from 9.72 crores in 1951 to 26.3 crores in 2011. However, in 2011, the ***number of cultivators declined for the first time and agricultural labourers increased.*** This is perhaps indicative of the shift of cultivators between 2001 and 2011 to non-agricultural activities. It is also possible that ***some cultivators may have joined the ranks of the landless labourers.*** [26]

Number of Cultivators and Labourers (in million)

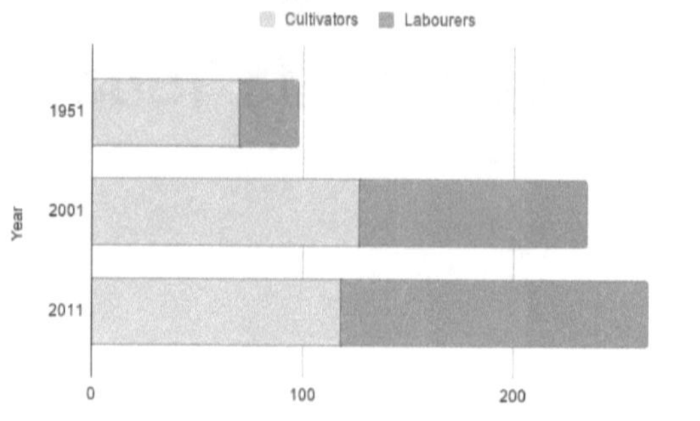

The number of farm labourers in the country increased by **3.75 crores** between 2001 and 2011 while the number of farmers reduced by **85 lakhs** during the same period.

Source: [26]

Nearly 90 lakh people migrated between states every year between 2011 and 2016 according to the Economic Survey of India 2016-17. [71] Census 2011 pegs the *total number of internal migrants in the country (accounting for inter- and intra-state movement) at a staggering 13.9 crores* with Uttar Pradesh and Bihar being the biggest source states. Nearly 1.06 crore migrants returned to their hometowns and villages during the March-April 2020 COVID induced lockdown. [119]

II. Agricultural Landholdings

According to the Agriculture Census 2015-16, the **average size of landholding is 1.08 hectares** and has been decreasing over the years. For male farmers, it is 1.10 and for female farmers, it is 0.90 ha. [27]

86% of the landholdings are in the small and marginal category, with landholding size less than 2 hectares. Consumption expenditure exceeds the income of farm households in this category (see bar graph). [26][27]

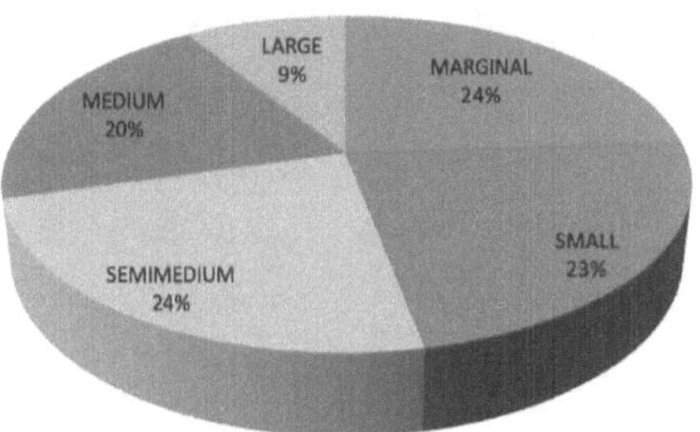

Source: [27]

Agricultural Household Budget by Landholding

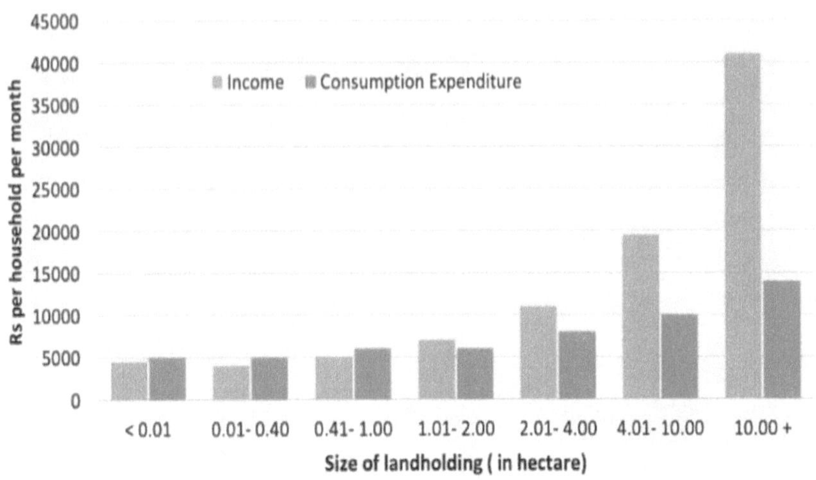

Source: [27]

III. Agricultural Incomes

- According to the report on 'Doubling Farmers' Income', [82] in 2015-16, the average yearly earning at current prices of a small and marginal farmer was ~Rs 80,000, of a medium and semi-medium farmer was ~Rs 2,01,000 and that of a large farmer (>10 ha) was three times more, at ~Rs 6,05,000.

- From 2002-03 to 2012-13, agricultural households registered an annual growth rate of 11.8% in their income on current prices and a mere 3.6% on constant prices. *A negative growth in real income* was observed in seven states and Union Territories. [82]

- The principle source of an agricultural household (AH)'s income is largely a function of the extent of land possessed. [26] Access to formal sources of credit is also directly correlated with the extent of land possessed. It also depends on the state they are located in. *High inequality in land distribution* stemming from colonial policies of land settlement and failed land reforms, have created this situation for a majority of smallholder households in India.

Relationship between poverty and agricultural income (Estimated by DFI committee from NSSO 70th Round unit level data).

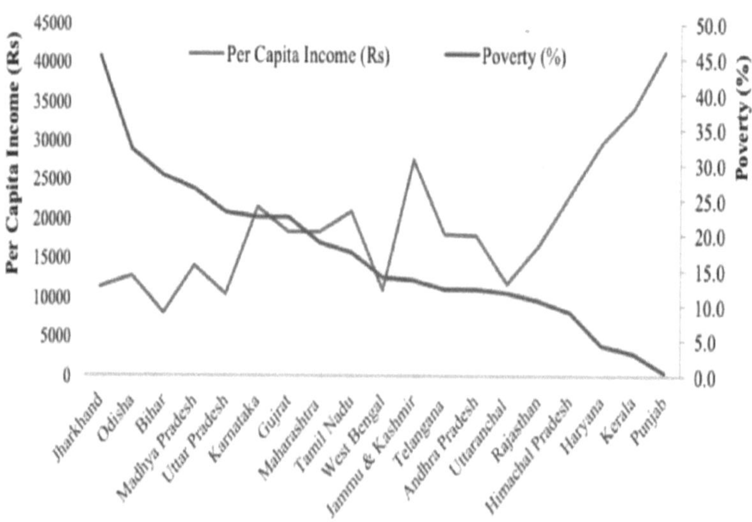

Source: [82] The graph shows that there is a correlation between the poverty ratio and per capita agricultural income of the listed states. In those states where agricultural income tends to be higher, poverty ratio tends to be lower.

According to the NSSO survey of agricultural households in 2012-13, nearly *one-third of income for agricultural households came from non-agricultural sources* including wage / salaried work and other forms of self-employment. [26]

Surprisingly, 35% of rural labour households reported that they owned some cultivated land. *Driven by pauperisation,* many land-owning households are forced to combine wage work with work on their own land. [113]

Percentage distribution of agrarian households by principle source of income

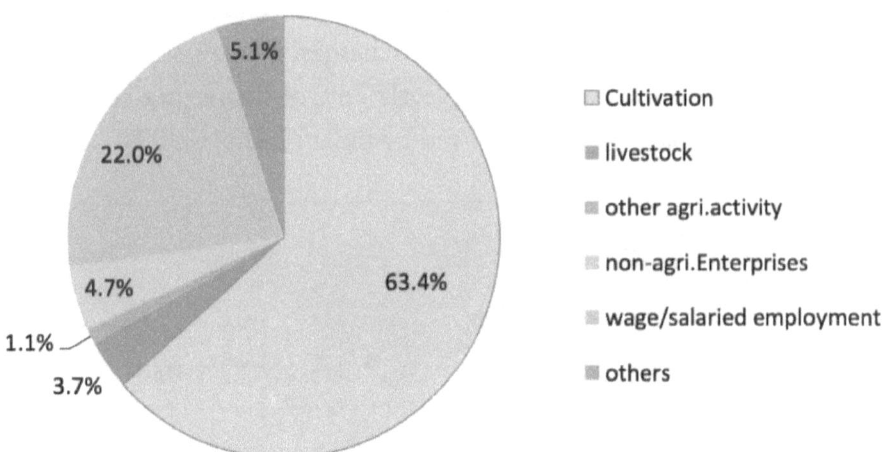

Source: [26]

In 2016-17, the NABARD Financial Inclusion Survey (NAFIS) found that the average monthly earning of an Agricultural Household was **Rs. 8931.** Of this, cultivation accounted for only **35%** and the rest was from other sources including wage labour (34%). [112]

Nearly **38%** of the agricultural households participating in NAFIS derived their household income from three or more sources. These households also had higher income compared to those who derived income from only one or two sources.

NAFIS also showed that only **48%** of rural households were agricultural households. Thus, the rural can no longer be equated with the agricultural.

IV. Tenant Farmers

- Tenant farmers and sharecroppers are cultivating a significant proportion of the land in many states – varying from 20% to 50%. But they are excluded from all government support systems due to lack of access to land titles including bank loans, crop insurance, disaster compensation and other schemes. Consequently they are *increasingly in the debt trap*. Nearly 75% of the farmer suicides in Telangana have been committed by tenant farmers. [29]

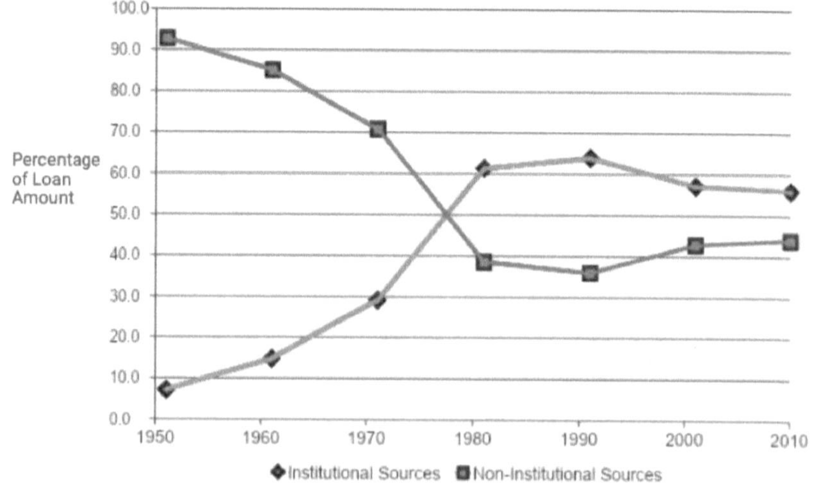

Source: [111]

V. Indebtedness

According to the Doubling Farmers' Incomes Report (2018), **52% of total agricultural households in India are under some form of debt** and the average size of the debt is Rs. 47,000. [26][41]

In the heartland of the Green Revolution, Punjab, the average debt of the agricultural households was Rs 1,19,500 in 2012-13, which was two-and-a-half times the all-India average. While 72% of the debt was from institutional sources, the remaining was owed to non-institutional sources like money-lenders, *arhtiyas* (commission agents), relatives or local traders. [41] [24]

According to the NAFIS 2016-17 survey, non-institutional sources accounted for **31%** of the outstanding loans of all rural households in 2016-17, while the share of banks stood at **47%** of the total outstanding loans. For agricultural households, the corresponding figures were **28%** (non-institutional sources) and **54%** (banks) respectively.

Only **10.5%** of agricultural households were found to have a valid KCC at the time of the NAFIS survey. [112]

VI. Rural Wages

- The national average daily wage rate for male and female field labour was Rs 315 and Rs 244 respectively in 2017-18. [95]
- There is wide scale inter-state variations with respect to daily wage rates as well as a gender based wage gap. Tamil Nadu had the highest (107%) while Himachal Pradesh had the lowest (7%) gender gap in wages in 2017-18. [95]

- The nominal average daily wage rates for unskilled labour in India increased from 2010-11 to 2017-18. However, the gender wage gap remained almost at the same levels. [25]
- In the case of skilled labour, Kerala had the highest daily wage rate of Rs 834 while Chhattisgarh has the lowest at Rs 282 in 2017-18. [95]

State-wise average daily wage rate of field labour (male) 2017-18

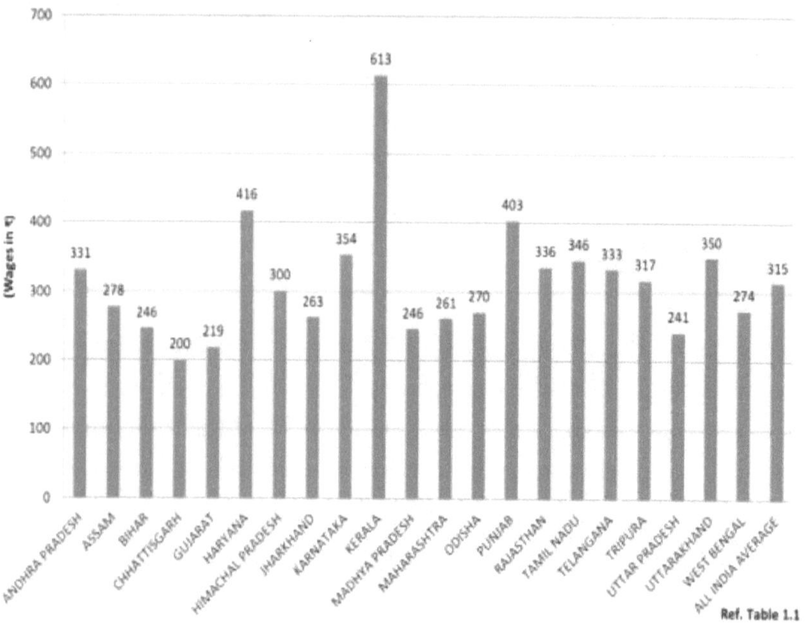

Source: [95]

State-wise average daily wage rate of field labour (female) 2017-18

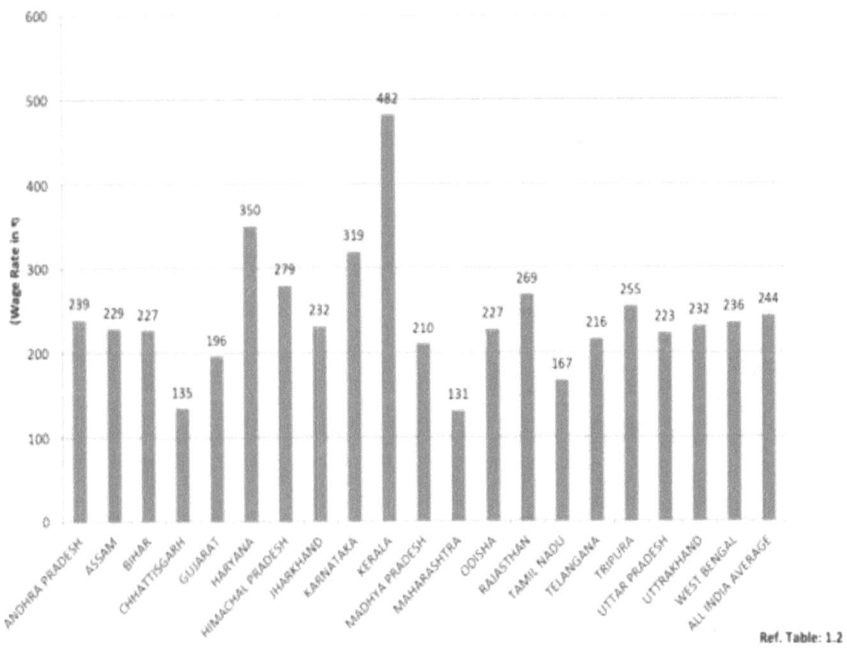

Source: [95]

Average daily wage rate for unskilled labour in India

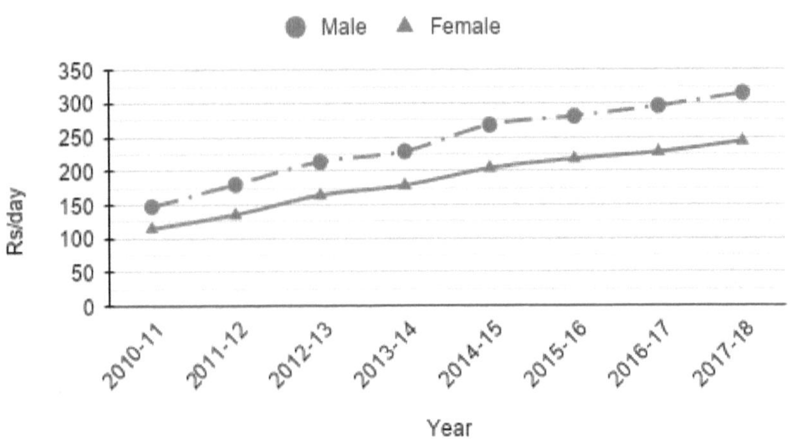

Source: [25]

Year on year growth rate of average daily nominal wage rates

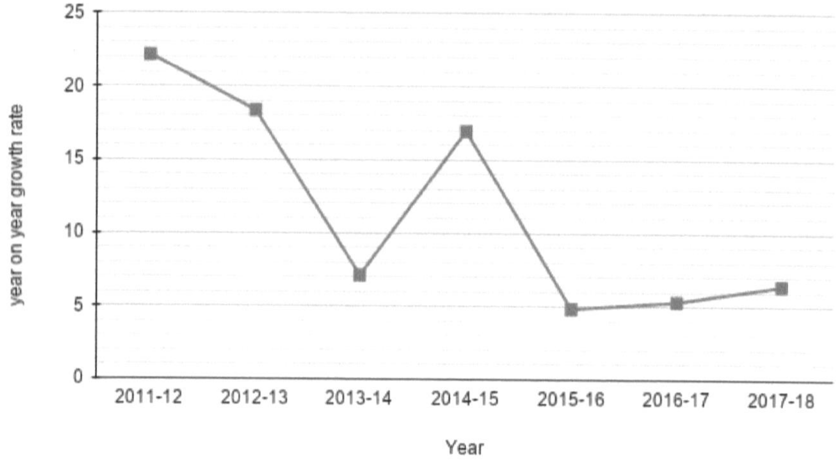

Source: [95]

VII. Rural Unemployment

- The rural unemployment rate has remained high throughout the last few years. In 2017-18 it was 4.9%, according to CMIE data. Before the COVID-19 related lockdown was imposed, the unemployment figure remained at a high of 7.3% and 8.4% in February and March 2020 respectively. With the COVID-19 induced lockdown it went up nearly three-fold to 23% in the months of April and May 2020. [81]

- The Periodic Labour Force Survey (PLFS) 2017-18 indicated that the rate of unemployment increased manifold between 2004-05 and 2017-18 as can be observed from the long green bars in the chart below.

Unemployment Rate in India

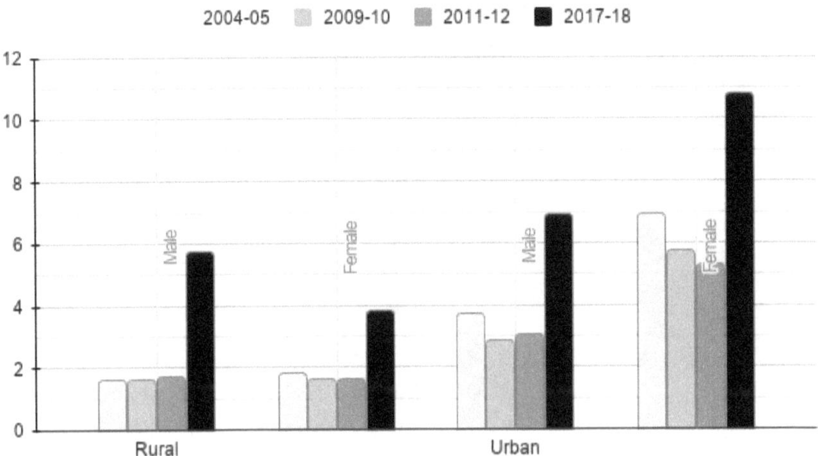

Source: [83]

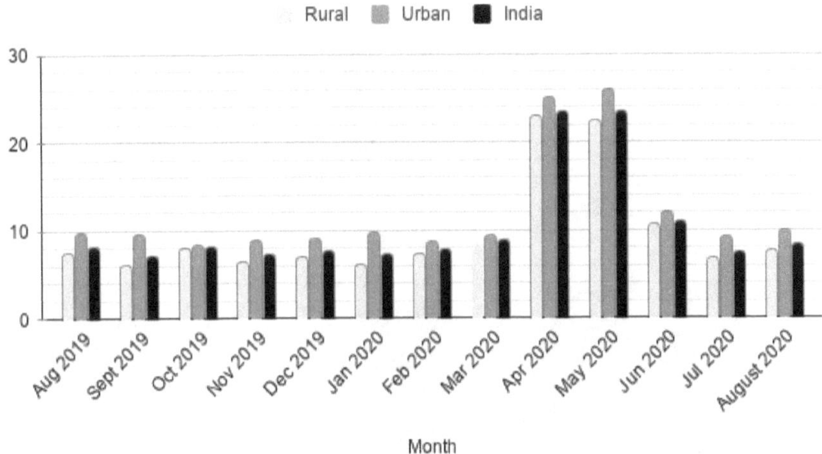

Source: [81]

VIII. Farmer Suicides

The 1990s saw the beginning of farmer suicides, affecting the most commercialised agricultural belts of the country, especially Punjab, Maharashtra, Karnataka, Andhra Pradesh, and various pockets in other states. According to official figures released by the National

Crime Records Bureau (NCRB), between 1995 and 2019 an average of 14,588 agriculturists committed suicide every year in India. [99] By the end of 2019, 3,64,692 agriculturists had committed suicide. [99][100][78]

5957 farmers and **4324** agricultural labourers committed suicide in 2019. The worst hit states were Maharashtra, Karnataka, Andhra Pradesh, Madhya Pradesh and Telangana. [100] NCRB data also states that from 2016 to 2019, the total number of suicides decreased from 11,379 to 10,281.*

*The accuracy of the latest figures is in question due to a number of reasons such as lack of coherence between data and media reports, lack of detail provided, arbitrary categorisations, and the extraordinarily long delay in the release of latest data. For instance, the data for 2016 came out in November 2019, and for 2017, 2018 and 2019 were released only in September 2020. Also, the NCRB data showed that West Bengal and Bihar reported zero suicides in 2016, but there were news reports stating otherwise. Further, detailed state-wise data has not been provided for 2017 and 2018, and from 2017 onwards, NCRB has also stopped stating the reasons for suicides such as crop failure, loans etc. [99][100]

IX. De-agrarianisation

A rural non-farm economic transformation has been taking place that involves:

a. a lesser share of rural households dependent on agriculture
b. households dependent on agriculture deriving a lesser share of income from agriculture and
c. a diversification largely into low end precarious employment outside agriculture.

Income from agriculture helps overcome the income shocks arising from the non-farm source of income, even as non-farm incomes provide a degree of insulation for agricultural households from the volatility of agrarian incomes. Given that access to the secure and well paying urban labour market is the only pathway out of such precarity, *aspirations for cultivating households are increasingly in the non-agrarian, non-rural space.*

X. Scheduled Caste Households

Accounted for 9% of all operational holdings. [27] Given that they made up 18.5% of the rural population (as per Census 2011), this meant slightly more than 50% of them were landless. [28]

61% of their holdings were less than 2 hectares in size compared to 46% for non-SC, non-ST communities. [28]

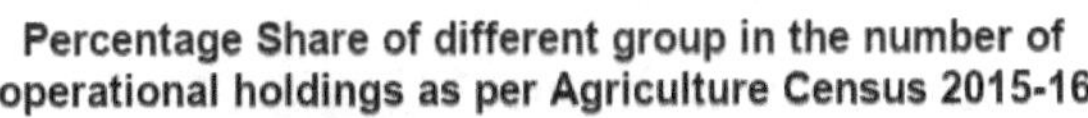
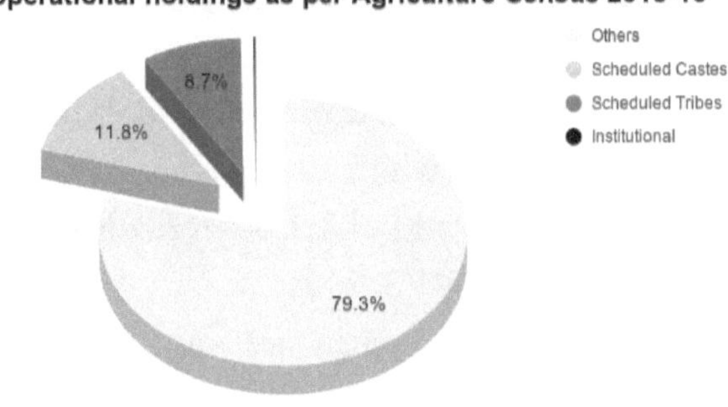

Source: [27]

XI. Scheduled Tribe Households

Accounted for 12% of all operational holdings. [27] Even though the average size of operational holdings is higher than the average in tribal areas, most of these landholdings lie in difficult terrain. Nearly 40% of them are small and marginal farmers. [28]

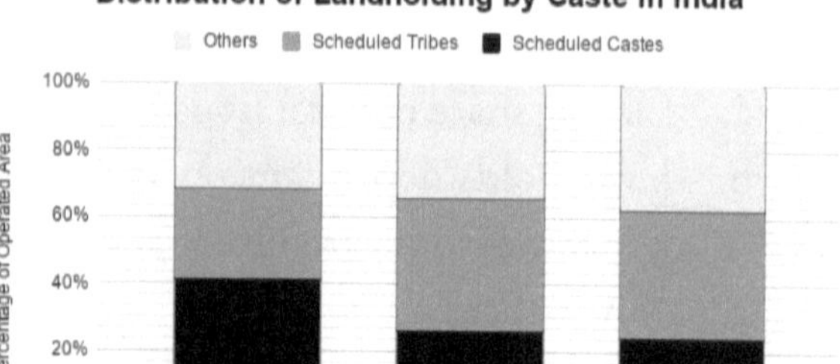

Source: [27]

All India average ratio of Net Irrigated Area to Net Sown Area is **46%** whereas for tribals it is half that, at **23%**. While **4%** of ST and **8%** of SC agricultural households owned tubewells, the percentage for OBCs and others was at **11.5%** and **19%** respectively. [112][70][29]

XII. Women Farmers

- According to the 2011 Census, 65.1% of the total female workforce in the country comprised of the agricultural workforce, which included 24% cultivators and 41.1% agricultural labourers. [84]

- Despite this, *women are not counted as 'farmers'* by government data collection sources since most women (86.5%) do not have land titles in their name. Such women, who do not own

land in their name but cultivate agricultural land, are counted as cultivators but not farmers. The 2011 Census counted 3.6 crore women as cultivators. [84][85]

- In the absence of formal recognition, these women 'cultivators' are *excluded from most government programs* such as eligibility for loans of various kinds, thereby, putting them into situations of vulnerability and insecurity on an everyday basis.

- The percentage share of female operational holders was 14% in 2015-16. [27] There exists a *substantial gap between men and women in the ownership, operation and management of agricultural assets.* Women's share of operational holdings also vary across states, with southern states such as Andhra Pradesh and Kerala showing relatively greater share of women. [84]

XIII. Allied Occupations

Pastoralists in India number about 3.4 crores managing a livestock of at least 5 crore. However, extensive sedentarization is occurring within pastoral groups due to difficulty in accessing forage, vanishing pastoral

grounds, increasing difficulty with pastoral mobility, lack of government support, exclusion of pastoralists from forest lands and suspicion by the wider settled society towards pastoralists. Pastoralists have traditionally been important keepers of diverse breeds of animals such as cattles, camels, goats, sheep etc. [54]

Fisheries are an important source of food, nutrition, employment and income in India. It provides livelihood to about 10.6 lakh fishers and fish farmers at the primary level and almost twice the number along the value chain. [72] However, mechanised trawling and single species aquaculture markets have devastated the coastal and ocean ecology with grave consequences for fishers.

Nearly 70% of all units in *Micro, Small and Medium Enterprises* (MSME) clusters are located in rural areas and over 90 per cent of these enterprises are microenterprises. Over 80% of the workers in rural MSMEs are informal workers. [3] They are not just artisanal, but have varying levels of mechanisation,

scales of and scope/diversity of manufacturing and markets. This reflects the rurality of unorganised manufacturing.

XIV. Loss of the Livestock Economy and Biodiversity

- A trend of reduction in livestock keeping due to a number of issues such as depletion of grazing lands, lack of access to natural resources, financial constraints, and labour issues has been observed. [86] The advent of mechanisation in farming and transport led to the breakdown of the integrated livestock-plant-soil production system and further dealt a blow to the livestock economy.

- Lack of financing for livestock rearing along with lack of community control over water bodies and commons due to increasing regulations have further impacted the occupation. Moreover, the promotion of milch breed exotic cattle varieties which are highly dependent on fodder crops has led to a conflict with food production for humans as well as caused *loss of species diversity*. [86]

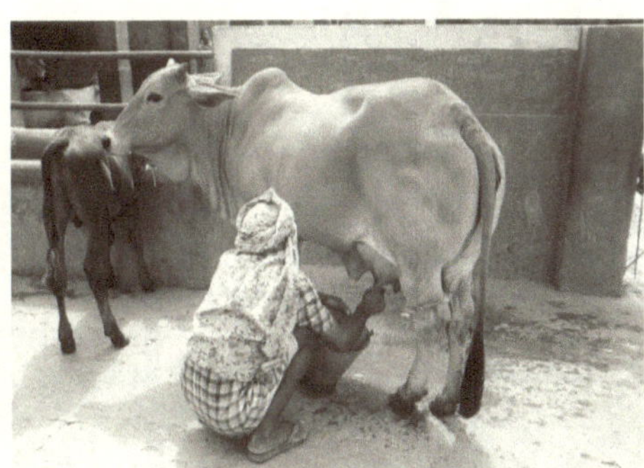

XV. Under-Nourishment

- With the dominant model's focus on supporting rice and wheat as the main cereal crops, at a national scale, the share of coarse cereals (millets - jowar, bajra, maize, and ragi) in cereal calories has declined from 23% in 1983 to 6% in 2011 for rural households, and from 10% to 3% in urban households. Because millets are relatively high in iron content, the decline in their consumption has led to an overall decrease in iron intake in cereals. This loss, combined with an overall decline in cereal consumption, has led to a net loss of iron in the average diet. The loss from millets was only partially compensated by rice, wheat, and other food groups. [22][12]

The share of coarse cereals (millets - jowar, bajra, maize, and ragi) in cereal calories has declined from **23%** in 1983 to **6%** in 2011 for rural households, and from **10%** to **3%** in urban households. Around **51.4%** women of reproductive age in India suffered from anaemia in 2016, which is the 2nd highest in South Asia.

- According to FAO, around **51.4%** *women of reproductive age in India suffered from anaemia in 2016*, which is the 2nd highest in South Asia. As per the Global Nutrition Report (2016) India is 170th out of 185 countries on prevalence of anaemia, which also affects 60% of children in the country. [23]

- The same report states that India ranks 114th out of 132 countries on under-5 stunting and 120th out of 130 countries on under-5 wasting. Stunting in children under five years of age was at 38% in 2015, which was much higher than the global average of 23%. [23]

XVI. Health Effects of Chemicalisation of Agriculture

- The Green Revolution's monoculture model led to greater use of pesticides, weedicides and fungicides on the farm. Farmers who spray pesticides in their fields themselves or through hired agricultural labourers suffer due to sickness, decreasing potential of work, economic loss due to health care costs and other *long term effects of pesticides on their health.* [56][74]

- Lack of awareness about the required dosage, re-entry period (minimum waiting time for chemicals to dissipate in the environment), protective gears and other safety measures, prove disastrous for the farmers, majority of whom are small and marginal. More dangerously, **contamination is biomagnifying** in the environment and in humans and animals.

- An epidemiological study of the agricultural community of Bathinda and Roop Nagar districts of Punjab lays the blame on pesticides, among other factors, for high rates of cancer prevalent there. [38] In Malwa region of Punjab, **cancer prevalence is directly correlated to farming** and gender, and the rate of prevalence is as high as 108.9 per crore per year as compared to the national average of 80 per crore per year. [20]

- ***Pesticide residues in food*** products also affect the health of consumers. [45] A recent study (2015) found a considerable potential of exposure to inorganic arsenic through consumption of rice. For an adult of 60 kg body weight, the maximum dietary risk of exposure to inorganic arsenic was calculated to be 1706% of the provisional tolerable weekly intake. [65]

Rate of cancer prevalence in the Malwa region of Punjab is as high as **108.9** per crore per year as compared to the national average of **80** per crore per year.

- The danger of high pesticide contamination in water and the environment led to the recent Anupam Verma Committee, constituted by the government, recommending that the use of ***13 pesticides should be banned, 27 pesticides should be reviewed*** in 2018 after completion of certain technical studies and 6 pesticides should be phased out by 2020. [68]
- The growing disease burden and ***rising healthcare costs*** have seriously impacted the vulnerable and marginalized sections in rural areas.

India has one of the most privatised healthcare systems in the world, with 80% of the health expenditure being financed through out-of-pocket expenses by households, often by incurring debt.

04 What Are the Conditions of Artisans in India?

I. Artisans

- A wide range of skilled artisans have been an integral part of rural India. According to the Working Group Report on Handicrafts for the 12th Five Year Plan (2012), there are nearly 70 lakh artisans in India. [51] Important artisanal occupations include weaving, carpentry, pottery, tannery, metal work, stone work, cane and bamboo work, jewellery making, wood carving, carpet making, zari work etc.

- According to the Dasra report (2013), around 63% of artisans are self-employed while 37% are wage earners. [118]

- Artisanal knowledge economies are structured around family, caste, and gender relations. An estimated 71% of artisans work as family units and 76% attribute their profession to the fact that they have learned family skills which are passed from one generation down to the next. [118]

- A majority of artisans belong to historically underprivileged communities according to the census of Handicrafts conducted in the 11th Plan. [103]

- During earlier times, their products were used as everyday objects, but with the coming of factory produced cheap products, the *demand for artisanal products has considerably reduced.*

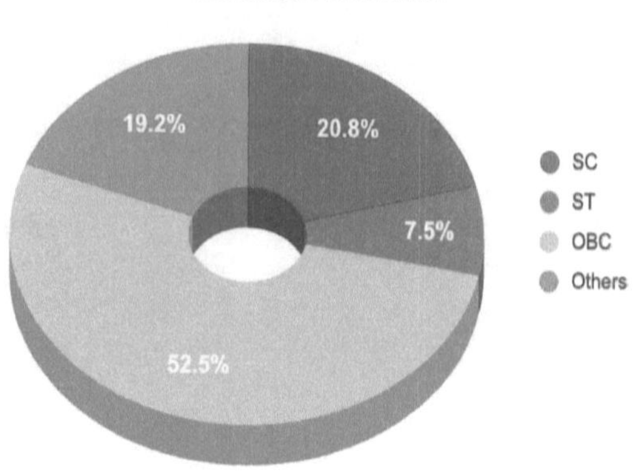

Source: [103]

II. Artisanal Occupations

- **Handloom weavers** have to increasingly compete with powerloom industries and mills. Inadequate credit facilities and increasing prices of the yarn mean that an ordinary weaver faces the barrier right at the point of entry into the production process. Rolling back welfare measures and reducing budgetary allocations has further aggravated the condition of handloom weavers. [53]

- **Leather workers** have been suffering from caste-related discrimination and atrocities over time. Recent closure of animal markets in many north and central Indian states has also negatively affected their sourcing of raw material, and competition from plastic footwear and other products has affected demand.

- **Pottery workers** have seen their products replaced with metal and then, plastic. Unavailability of uncontaminated, good quality mud is another source of concern.

III. Problems Faced by Artisans

- Formal education policies drawing upon a **modernisation paradigm that over-values speed, efficiency and standardisation** have led to a devaluation of artisanal skills and knowledge as 'traditional' and 'backward' and pushed them into precarity. Efforts to revive these skills have broadly remained within the paradigm of preservation, rather than working towards a creative blend of artisanal technologies with modern ones to ensure that such skills are not devalorised.

- On the demand side, the shift of consumers away from their products due to the **availability of cheap substitutes** has led to declining incomes and on the supply side, a lack of raw materials due to **disappearance of commons** such as water-bodies and pasture land, and **contamination of raw materials** such as sand has been a source of problems.

- Artisanal products have been appreciated worldwide for their aesthetics, techniques as well as far lesser ecological footprint as compared to industrially produced goods. However, the **industrialising paradigm treats artisans as relics of the past** and refuses to recognise artisanal work as a viable livelihood. Current educational systems also do not recognise the value of such knowledge forms.

- Artisanal skills are caste based and there have been **no policy measures to democratise such skills**. Instead, by tying up artisanal promotion to preservation of the caste order, policies have indirectly affirmed a caste based division of labour.

 What constitutes the Web of Risks in Agriculture?

- An important component of the Green Revolution model of high-input, high productivity agriculture in its initial years was the ***public-funded farm extension system providing knowledge support to farmers.*** The success of the Green Revolution firmly established this model in which the national agricultural research system became the source of all agricultural knowledge and the indigenous knowledge systems of the farming communities were completely marginalised.

- Rather than drawing upon the knowledge and vast experience of the farming communities and other stakeholders or building upon local agro-ecological characteristics for choosing cropping patterns, the agricultural science establishment plunged headlong into pushing high yielding crop varieties and inputs in a centralised manner. This process ***re-configured diverse ecologies and cast them into irrigated landscapes growing few crops.*** This contributed to the web of risks.

Heavy centralization of agricultural science and technology research

Knowledge Dissonance and Technological Treadmills

Hunger, the Green Revolution and GMOs

Heavy Centralization of Agricultural Science and Technology Research

- It included both, a ***centralization of setting research agendas*** (irrigation - chemicals - HYVs) and the centralisation and consolidation of research funding (over 80% was allocated to Indian Council of Agricultural Research (ICAR) institutes). State Governments and respective State Agricultural Universities were neglected and the meagre funding they received was also tied to research content.

- The complete buy-in of the agricultural science establishment to an already formulated policy goal of ***improving grain productivity at any cost*** ruled out all forms of alternatives from being tried out, even at a small scale, within the establishment. The singular achievement of raising food production placed this monoculture, high productivity model more firmly on a pedestal.

- Further, there was ***no effective dialogue between the natural and social sciences*** so that robust and holistic scientific research could be done effectively. [42]

- ***Uniform education and accreditation mechanisms*** (in a country with explosive agricultural diversity) and universalisation of the hierarchical 'Package of Practices' system (from the state to farmers), further contributed to devaluing local knowledge and biodiversity.

- For instance, national level standardised systems of evaluating and understanding soils, through programs like the soil health card, are ill-equipped to assess the problem of soils at the micro level of the agro-ecosystem. They fail to look at the soil as a living system. Much of our formal scientific research on soils has also sidestepped the issue of interlinkages between the physical, biological and the chemical, and instead, chosen to focus on narrow singular factors affecting soils. [42]

National level standardised systems of evaluating and understanding soils fail to look at the **soil as a living system**. Much of our formal scientific research on soils has also sidestepped the issue of interlinkages between the physical, biological and the chemical, and instead, chosen to focus on narrow singular factors affecting soils.

5.2   Knowledge Dissonance and Technological Treadmills

- The scaling down of extension services by the state with liberalisation in the 1990s adversely impacted the flow of information to farmers [26] and increased **dissonance in knowledge.** [30]
- The poor performance of the state-funded extension and increasing competition among agri-business players led to a situation where these agri-business companies and traders assuming the role of **suppliers of both knowledge and inputs** to the farmers. The intense rivalry between farmers to out-compete each other has led to the wide use of new commercial varieties of seeds, fertilizers, and pesticides, which has also led to increasing 'agricultural **deskilling'.** [30]
- **Caste, class and gender** have shaped access to information and often, only large, male, upper caste farmers have access to the scientific and bureaucratic establishment and its flow of knowledge and inputs. Others are increasingly **dependent on input dealers** and suppliers who are more inclined to promote products with the highest financial returns as opposed to efficacy in the field. [73]

Spurious pesticides accounted for 25% by value (Rs. 3200 crores in 2013) and 30% by volume of the domestic pesticide industry as per a pan-India study by FICCI in 2015. Weak law enforcement and failure of the public and private extension systems were seen as the primary culprits. [26]

- All these magnified the web of risks, especially for farmers in dryland areas of the country and for those belonging to underprivileged castes and classes. Agriculturists found themselves unable to provide for their families as they attempted to sustain themselves within this dominant model.

- Along with the technological treadmill, increasing indebtedness, lack of marketing support, and unviable parcels of land made agriculture a losing proposition. This was especially the case for those with inadequate capital, knowledge and support and who considered this to be the only route to enhancing their livelihoods, economic mobility and social status. In such a context of risks (and burdens of debt), loss of production meant that the loss became a deeply personalized loss of self, often leading to suicide. [30]

Technological Treadmill, increasing indebtedness, lack of marketing support, and unviable parcels of land have made agriculture a losing proposition.

5.3 Hunger, the Green Revolution and GMOs

- The Green Revolution was justified by the argument that India had a serious *food production deficit in the 1960s* and was importing huge quantities of food from other countries to meet its needs. The image of the Great Bengal Famine of 1943 was often invoked to legitimise the promotion of grain productivity programs and capital-technology-chemical inputs into agriculture as ways to prevent famines.

- However, re-examination of the experience of the 1943 Bengal Famine by Amartya Sen has shown that the famine was not due to unavailability of food but due to *lack of entitlements* of the poor. Enough food was available but people could not afford to purchase it, and hence, went hungry. [91] Moreover, food imports were not due to unavailability of food domestically but due to  geopolitical considerations and domestic concerns about moving food from surplus states to deficit states.

- It is also to be noted that in the decade that immediately followed independence (1950-60), there was a remarkable recovery in the performance of agriculture. That decade saw the highest increase in productivity across all crops. [76] Even after the adoption of the Green Revolution paradigm, **hunger did not disappear**, as a large portion of the population could not afford to purchase enough

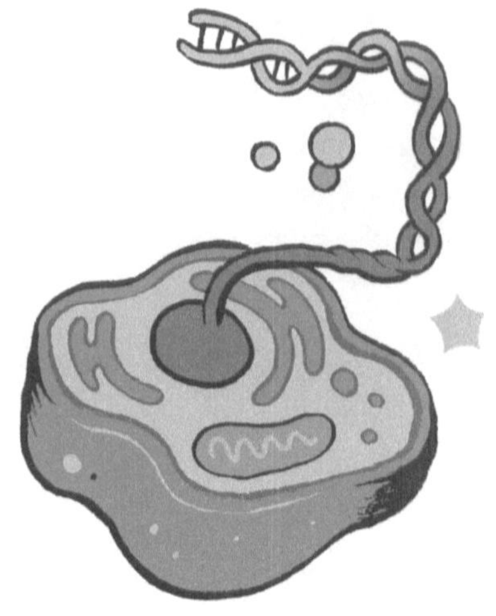

food. Moreover, we lost the diversity of our farms and the nutrition of our plates. **Genetically Modified (GM) crops follow the same logic of monoculture** farming, replicating the known problems of pest resistance that plagued farmers in the Green Revolution. [17] Further, neither of the two principal GM traits commercialized globally, insect resistance and herbicide tolerance, enhance yields.

- GM crops have been promoted in the name of feeding the growing world population, especially the billions of poor. Research on statistics that have been used to calculate the **'food' required to feed a global population of 9 billion in 2050** shows that a far greater proportion of that food is destined to feed the much smaller population of the global north. This is because of the projected sustained growth of meat consumption in the global north that would require far more land, water and energy to produce. [93]

- Unfortunately, world over we are saddled with global and national food systems that leave **millions food insecure** and generate significant collateral damage in the form of environmental degradation. [92]

What are the Perils of Populism and the State's Role in This?

- *Public investment* was the key driver of the Green Revolution. *Active state support* including high subsidies for inputs (seeds, fertilisers, electricity, water, pesticides) and purchasing their output at a guaranteed MSP were an essential part of the package. The state also made public investments in irrigation infrastructure, rural electrification, agricultural markets, agricultural extension, public distribution of food, provision of cheap agricultural credit through formal institutions, and investment in agricultural research.

- However, these subsidies and price incentives were given only for wheat and later, rice and sugarcane, which led to farmers shifting to these crops massively. [63][64] This *distorted the cropping pattern* by promoting irrigated crops in dryland areas and also affected people's health by reducing the diversity of foods on our plate and replacing them with highly polished rice, wheat and the empty calories of refined sugar. [22]

- Drawing upon the tenets of development economics for the modernisation of agriculture, these incentives to produce more food were originally designed to 'bet on the strong'. Not surprisingly, there was a *disturbing skew in the kinds of farmers who benefitted*--only those who were able to afford irrigation

were able to grow these crops--typically, upper caste farmers and those from the other backward classes in the irrigated heartland. Farmers in the drylands and hilly regions, growing millets, pulses, oilseeds, and other crops did not receive any such benefits from the government. Thus, public investment in agriculture contributed to *growing inequality* across the country.

- These *social and ecological costs of the subsidy and price policy* need to be recognised.

- In recent years, the government started purchasing pulses and some millets at MSP which has led to increase in their acreage. The demand from farmers and civil society organisations is for the government to purchase all crops at MSP so that all farmers get the same price guarantee. However, it is impractical for the government to be a buyer of last resort for all crops. Such policies have to be firmly based on the idea of diversifying the cropping system and not incentivising and promoting new forms of monocultures. Identification of *crops that are ecologically suited to each region* must be carefully assessed and promoted.

6.1 Minimum Support Prices, Loan Waivers, and State Investment in Agriculture

I. Minimum Support Prices and Loan Waivers

- *Populism* refers to catering to the interests of those who have presence or power, especially vis-à-vis the state. In India, agrarian populism is marked by the state *giving in to the demands of farmers* who have medium or large landholdings, who are from the *dominant castes and have political power*. Much of it is linked to retaining their political alliances.

- It is these farmers who have primarily benefited from the MSP regime. However, the technological treadmill and rising input costs have forced them to agitate for higher minimum support prices since the 1980s. Even today, the rise in MSP to cover the cost of cultivation (C2 costs) is one of the major arguments of the farmer movements in India.

- Even though this has put the government in difficult situations because of the *growing subsidy burden* and *overflowing stocks* of wheat and rice in government godowns (since the 1980s), successive governments have responded with populist measures and increased MSP year after year. This has primarily benefited a select group of comparatively better-off farmers, with complete disregard for the social and ecological costs of the policy.

- Further, in the last two decades, state investment has shifted away from public or community based investment in agriculture (e.g. water management, markets, soil health) to other *populist policies* in the short term such as loan waivers, insurance, and income support, directed at individual cultivators. For instance, it subsidised sprinkler equipment rather than investing in watershed management.

- However, populist policies like a moratorium on loans or subvention of interest rates are quick-fixes and not the real solutions. Even after the loan waiver, if external input-intensive farming practices continue unhindered, farmers will be forced into *debt year after year due to rising input costs.*

X. State Investment in Agriculture

The following two graphs show the variation in agricultural subsidies and public investment from 1981 to 2013 in Rupees (100 crores)

Agriculture Expenditure and Input Subsidies (Rupees in 100 crores at 2004-05 prices)

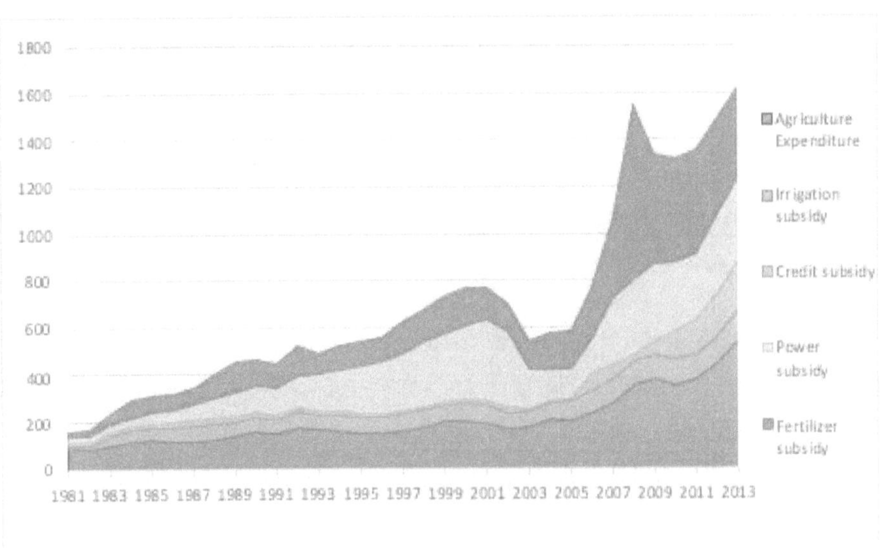

Source: [46]

Input Subsidies and Public Investment (Rupees in 100 crores) Source: [46]

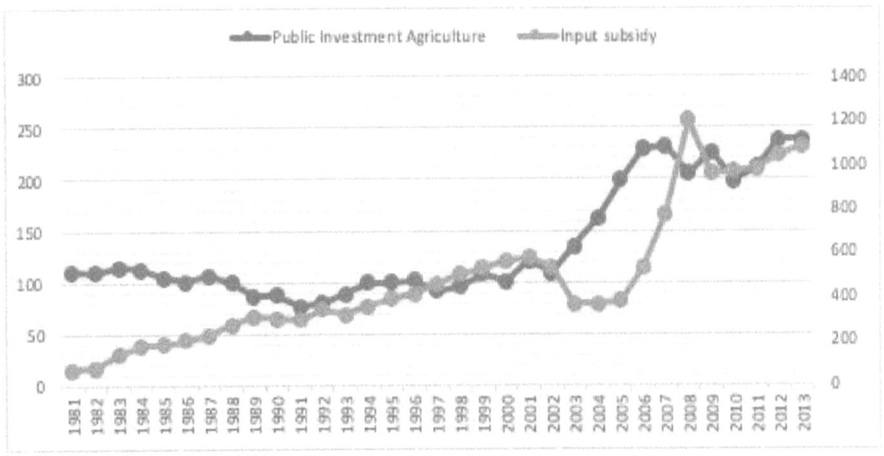

Almost 90% of public capital formation / investment in the early years of the Green Revolution went to building the fertiliser industry and irrigation infrastructure. [2] Under the garb of populism, the state has spent much more on "industrial subsidies" for agriculture, than on farmers.

During the period 1990 to 2010, less than 0.4% of agricultural GDP was allocated to agricultural research (excluding education expenditure) while input subsidies alone accounted for between 8% and 11% of agricultural GDP. [14][34] In 2006-07, input subsidies accounted for 88% of the total plan outlay for agriculture, irrigation and rural development. [13] In 2014-15, subsidies on fertilisers (3.4%), power (2.59%) and irrigation (1.48%) together accounted for about 7.47% of the GDP originating in agriculture and allied activities. [1]

6.2 Lack of Accountability in Agricultural Markets

- The *Agricultural Produce Marketing Committee (APMC) Act* that set up the public market yard (*mandi*) infrastructure of the country in the 1970s was created with the intention of curtailing the power of agricultural intermediaries (traders, brokers, processors, etc.). However, over time, the APMC mandis came to be **controlled by a handful of trading families** in many places, creating oligopolies over finance, trade, processing and transport. Lack of downward accountability, conflicts over quality determination and weighment, and structural constraints faced by farmers (such as interlinked credit and product markets, small lot sizes of varying quality, crashing prices with local oversupply), plagued the marketing process.

- For the majority of small and marginal farmers, transportation costs to the mandi were prohibitive and they sold at the village itself to local traders who paid them less.

- Post-liberalisation in the 1990s, price volatility, growth of agribusinesses, and other factors, led the central and state governments to promote online commodity futures markets, contract farming, direct purchase by corporates from the farmers and private marketplaces, where farmers could sell their produce.

- However, in private market yards, *companies set their own rules for purchase (especially regarding quality)* and didn't hold an auction, since they were the sole buyer. Farmers had very little ability to influence the rules or negotiate in the private marketplace, unlike the *public mandi space where farmers could collectively demand accountability* from officials and had the option to make complaints against traders. Companies were primarily accountable to shareholders, not farmers. [75]

- Recently, the government has passed the 'The Farmers' Produce Trade And Commerce (Promotion And Facilitation) Act, 2020' to effectively *bypass the mandi system.* However, APMC markets have been an important medium for price discovery at the local level for the farmers and their dismantling will leave farmers with no buyer of last resort. The need has been to *reform the mandis and improve their accountability towards farmers,* not bypass them altogether. [39]

- For instance, the repeal of the APMC Act in Bihar, back in 2006, neither helped farmers who have been forced to distress sell their produce year after year, well below the MSP, nor has it been able to ensure private investment in the development of market yards. [31]

- Further, participation in online commodity futures markets and negotiable warehouse receipts *requires a certain lot size*, which is beyond the ability of 90% of farmers in the country. These institutions have been used mostly by traders and agribusinesses rather than farmers. [75][76]

- Contract farming has also got a boost with the 'The Farmers (Empowerment and Protection) Agreement on Price Assurance and Farm Services Act, 2020'. However, given the power hierarchy between farmers and big-pocket sponsors, the terms of the contract and the possibility of its enforcement are skewed in favour of the latter. Also, large investments by a few corporates into crops that meet urban and global demand would *adversely impact the already skewed crop diversity* in the country. [31] This integration into long supply chains would also create transportation emissions, negatively impacting the climate.

6.3 Can e-National Agricultural Marketplace (e-NAM) Help?

- The government also started the e-National Agricultural Marketplace (e-NAM) to link mandis all over the country on a single online platform, which would enable price discovery and facilitate transactions. [36] However, movement of agriculture produce continues to happen through mandis, and integration with e-NAM depends on the physical development of enabling infrastructure in markets, especially linked to quality determination, logistics and transportation. Only half the mandis are connected with e-NAM to date and *only one-third have quality certification in place.* [36]

- Moreover, the *process of quality certification is not only time-consuming but also expensive* and thus, out of reach for most farmers.

- Although e-NAM trades in 150 commodities, in almost all cases only a single commodity has been taken up for e-NAM trading in each mandi and even that is done on an optional basis. Inter-mandi and inter-state trade is yet to materialise. [39]

- Research in Karnataka's mandis, which was the first state to unify their markets but has not joined e-NAM, shows that in the absence of competition from outside traders, the *new electronic system is as vulnerable as before to the threat of local collusion,* with instances of bids placed around those of the dominant trader, boycotts against e-trading, the moving of commodities to non-e-trading days, and movement of trading outside the mandi in non-registered transactions. [39] Commission agents are responsible for unloading, entering the bid for, and making the payment for a farmer's lot. They continue to retain influence over the system in being able to delay payments for farmers. But they are also necessary to amalgamate multiple farmers' lots for creating a minimum lot size to be able to participate in the e-NAM.

> Although e-NAM trades in **150 commodities**, in almost all cases **only a single commodity** has been taken up for **e-NAM** trading in each mandi and even that is done on an optional basis.

- Moreover, mandis with good infrastructure and grading facilities are also the most competitive and provide a suitable marketing environment for farmers. Linking those very mandis to e-NAM does nothing to fix the infrastructure and oligopolistic environment of other mandis in the country. Thus, core problems faced by farmers in agricultural marketing would not be addressed through e-NAM.

- Further, without *allied interventions in input and credit markets*, an online trading platform cannot transform market exchange and make it competitive. Rather than disintermediation, which is a misguided goal, the need is to *make marketing institutions accountable* to farmers and address the constraints in other, inter-linked markets also. [39]

- Ultimately, e-NAM can be a portal to help traders find markets for the produce they have amalgamated and it could help link processors, millers, wholesalers, corporate sellers and buyers, and other intermediaries in the supply chain; but it holds out little hope for farmers in its current form.

07 What Are the Implications of Corporate Control, Intellectual Property Regimes, and Datafication of Agriculture?

I. Corporate Control

- Post liberalisation there has been greater corporate control of parts of the agricultural supply chain from inputs to output in India. The top four corporations: Bayer-Monsanto, ChemChina-Syngenta, DOW-Dupont and BASF *control 70% of inputs such as commercial seeds* and a large proportion of agrochemicals in the country. [37] Also, there is growing consolidation in the edible oil sector and increasing corporate interest in food marketing and retail.

- Internationally, corporations control almost the entire seed germplasm in cotton, soya, and canola, which is genetically modified. They also control the production and trade of agrochemicals, farm machinery, and processing, commodity trading and retail (supermarkets) operations (Big Four - ADM, Bunge, Cargill, Louis Dreyfus). Recent mergers and acquisitions have created *global behemoths controlling seed and agrochemical businesses* (Monsanto-Bayer, ChemChina-Syngenta, Dow-Dupont) corporations. It is almost impossible for governments to hold such large and powerful financial entities accountable for their actions.

- Free Trade Agreements have benefitted many of these companies as they have operations in multiple countries and can take advantage of price fluctuations and large inventory stocks.

- Corporatisation of agriculture and food production has also led to the establishment of 'factory farms' in the case of animals, which, as recent studies indicate, are the sources of new diseases and epidemics. [11]

II. Intellectual Property Rights on Seeds and Plant Varieties

- The paradigm of intellectual property whose rules are set by transnational actors *does not give due recognition to the innovation by farmers* such as locally developed seeds or adapted varieties.

- The rural, in such a scenario, becomes a space from which both genetic materials and local knowledge are borrowed to be 'innovated' somewhere else in urban centres and then *sold back to the farmers*. [80]

- This not only leads to higher input costs for farmers, but also results in the corporate control of agriculture.

III. Techno-Financial Regimes, Digitalisation and Datafication of Agriculture

- Increasing financialisation of natural resources (*land, seeds, risk have all become commodities*) and growing digitalisation of such transactions (cash transfers and biometric authentication) are now shaping rural India. Land is more valuable as real estate and even fertile agricultural land, along with water bodies, wetlands, grasslands that have been classified as unculturable 'wasteland' are being converted into concrete plots.

- Digitalisation of transactions is seen to bring transparency but *privacy of data is a growing concern*. It is also eroding past relationships based on social capital and trust that ensured a minimal form of social security for people. Hence, adoption of the modern technological tools and instruments must entail a cautionary approach. [89]

- It has also become possible today to collect micro-level farm data using drones and other digital technologies. The data collected is fed into Artificial Intelligence based systems to glean information regarding input requirements, crop types etc. The claim is that digital technologies will support precision agriculture which would in turn result in better productivity.

- However, as has been observed from the story of Green Revolution, these technologies might *create a situation of dependency among farmers and corporatisation of agriculture.* [90] It is also unclear whether these technologies can support small scale, diversified and agroecologically suitable cropping systems or are suitable and affordable only for large scale monoculture farms, which are also ecologically unsustainable. Therefore, the need is to explore the short, medium and long term implications of datafication of agriculture.

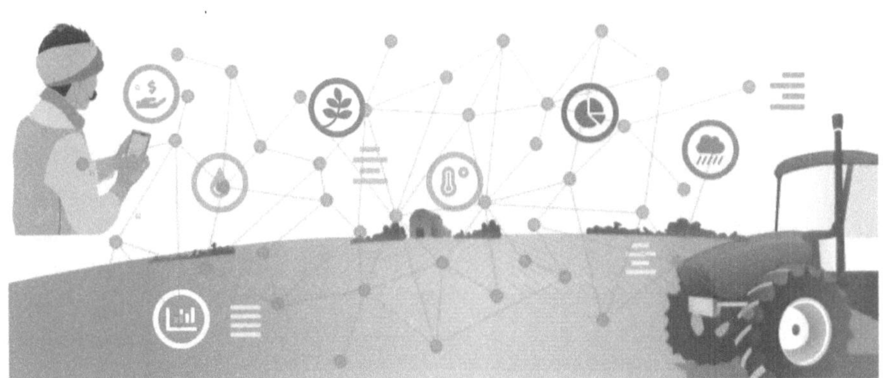

08 Alternative Visions for Rural India: Guiding Principles

I. Environmental Sustainability and Interdependence

Rural policies have to be re-imagined with social justice and environmental sustainability at the core. We must recognise agriculture and the rural as being part of a larger ecosystem and realise that co-existence or interdependence is the fundamental premise underlying the natural world. Agroecology, with its scientific core, as well as local, experiential understandings of how we can work with nature instead of against it, are the guiding principles in this endeavour. [14][57][58]

II. Take Climate Change Seriously

The climate emergency is here and we must move away from economic models that encourage growth based on high consumption. There are ecological limits to growth and social challenges related to inequality in access to resources, which must be urgently recognised by our policy intelligence.

III. The Rural and the Non Rural Together in a Circular Economy Framework

The current extractive relationship of the economy with the environment, where the latter is a source of raw materials, food and labour, and a dumping ground for waste, must be changed. Moving beyond the old-mindset shaped by the ideas of modernisation, industrialisation and economic development, production and consumption systems and practices must be reshaped in the form of "circular economies."

IV. New Indicators and Metrics of Measuring Success

The outcomes of these alternative policy frameworks cannot be assessed using conventional indicators. We need new ones. We must change our measurements – what is counted and what is left out – if we wish to address structural issues of both, the rural, in general, and agriculture, in particular. We cannot continue to valourise consumption driven growth and increasing GDP. We must resurrect the value of nature's bounty and human labour.

V. Reimagine The Rural as a Positive Space for Meaningful Livelihoods

Adverse integration of the rural within the project of modernity and development, and the promotion of industrial products, has made much of the rural irrelevant. The vast diversity of people and occupations in the rural space, within and outside of agriculture has been marginalised. Given that the urban, industrial transition narrative has only led to growing unemployment and jobless growth, this perspective will have to change. The rural cannot be made redundant. Work that has been ecologically suitable, meaningful and satisfying cannot be discarded and demeaned as 'backward', 'traditional', 'low status', but supported as a critical source of livelihood.

VI. Decentralisation of Policy Making

Decision making has to be collective, inclusive, democratic and transparent. Policymaking cannot be confined to the hallowed spaces of Delhi and state capitals, but has to come down to where the people, especially the 'marginalised majority', are and address their issues and concerns. [94] However, while we recognise the importance of decentralised policy making to the scale of agro-ecological regions, it is important to begin with restoring the policy making authority of state governments which is being eroded. Further, state governments should foster more decentralised policy institutions that are networked across spatial scales for learning, design and implementation, with knowledge and values emerging from an interaction between the global and the local.

What Are the Types of Climate Preparedness and Climate Resilient Initiatives?

I. Promote Ecologically Appropriate Agriculture

- Climate related risk mitigation and preparation needs to focus on promoting varied ecologically appropriate agricultural practices and livelihood options, especially recognising the interlinkages between livestock, plants and the local ecology.
- Natural resources such as rivers, lakes, tanks, aquifers, grazing grounds, forests and green cover must be conserved.
- Commons – wetlands, grasslands, scrub forests, river banks, ponds, lakes, streams, rivers – must be rejuvenated and locally managed with adequate representation of various social groups. Food and nutritional security should be derived not only from the diversity of cultivated foods (going beyond quantity alone) but also include uncultivated and wild foods from the commons.

II. Build Local and Regional Scientific Research Capacity to Tackle Climate Change

- Decentralise the national agricultural research system and encourage the involvement of local stakeholders (farmers, processors, traders, consumers, policymakers, government officials, etc.) in suggesting priorities for research.

- Incentivise agricultural scientists and those in allied natural and social science disciplines to build local capacity for scientific research, building on a climate-friendly research agenda.
- There is a need to develop an early warning system with growing cycles being affected, new pests and diseases emerging and pathogens mutating with the advent of climate change.

III. Recognise Ecological Services

- The ecological services of natural resources and of farming practices that conserve resources should be recognised and remunerated. Projects that erode and devastate local ecologies must be stopped or penalised. [8]

IV. Value Variability

- The diversity of nature must be protected and supported as a strategy for risk management in the face of climate change.
- Over emphasis on grain productivity of few crops and few varieties (whether high yielding, hybrid or genetically modified) must be replaced with the promotion of research on multiple varieties and crops that work together in a given agroecological system.
- Local knowledge and practices of cultivation that thrive and work with the variability of nature (monsoons, pests, diseases, other ecological conditions) must be recognised and valued.

V. Push for a Responsive and Decentralised Administration

- Management of resources (such as water, electricity and cooking gas/source) must be decentralised so that there is local accountability and care for these resources.
- Price incentives of the Public Distribution System (PDS) should be modified to encourage crops like millets and pulses.

- The PDS should allow for *decentralised grain banks* that store and distribute local food grains. This will promote the cultivation of local foods, retain local food cultures, and also cut costs of transportation and management in an excessively centralised system. This is being done successfully to support hitherto neglected crops like millets and pulses in Odisha and Karnataka.

- The extension system would need to be overhauled to *bring on board local and experiential knowledge* of cultivation practices suited to agroecology and climatic concerns, along with scientific inputs. Continuous upgradation of skills would be a must, given changing environmental conditions and advent of new technologies. It would also need to be accountable, and its impact, measurable.

- The agricultural science establishment must articulate its own legitimate scientific voice in collaboration with other relevant stakeholders in society (in a decentralized and democratic manner) to pursue the goal of sustainability and resilience in farming, especially in the light of major social and ecological disruption due to agricultural production technologies and increasing climate variability and change. [42][67]

- There is an urgent need to develop and promote a range of appropriate technologies for agriculture and rural industries. The current promotion of heavy and extractive technologies are compounding the economic and ecological crises.

- There is a need to move away from a purely monetary / cash flow income subsidy regime (given to individuals) to a *system of public and private investments* through communities or local groups that will regenerate rural livelihoods in water, soils, markets, seeds, crafts etc.

- Ensuring functioning, quality public health and educational services will go a long way in enhancing the well-being of rural citizens.

VI. Challenge Intellectual Property Rights and Corporatisation of Agriculture

- There is a need to promote legal pluralisms and move away from singular policies for all places, while taking on board agrobiodiversity and ecological difference. This is especially concerning international and national seed policy and its implications for biodiversity.

- This would mean challenging the basic assumptions behind notions of regulatory coherence and standardisation of laws, of sites, and of knowledge forms.

- There is a need for a *new framework for community resources* like water, wetlands, rivers, and other common resources, including a provision for community rights (without reifying the community and recognising deep hierarchies of knowledge and power within communities).

- This would mean confronting and *challenging the extreme privatisation of commons*, resources like seeds, and investments in agricultural research and markets. The consolidation of private control through mergers and acquisitions across domains like

seeds, agrochemicals, processing and retail and in global value chains must also be challenged.

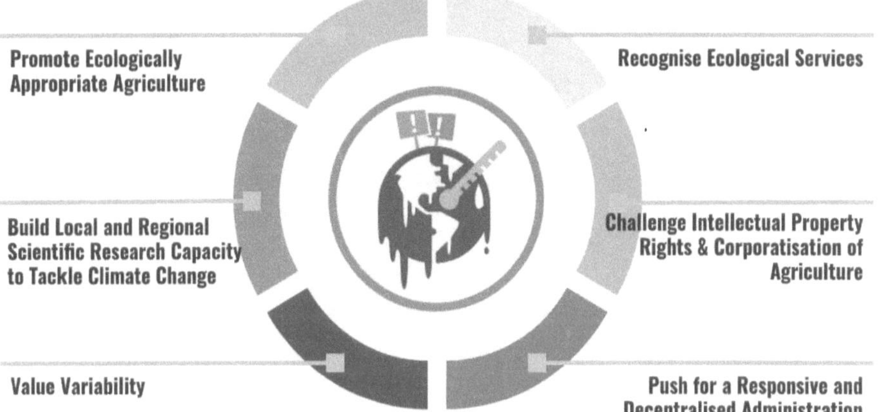

10 How Can We Revive and Strengthen Varied Rural Economies?

I. Going Beyond the Safety Net of MGNREGS

- The dispossession of workers from agriculture and artisanal occupations with the coming of technology based production systems has not resulted in their being absorbed into other livelihoods in rural or urban areas. The Mahatma Gandhi National Rural Employment Guarantee Scheme has been a safety net for rural workers in the last 15 years, as a welfarist response from the government. [49]

- The growth of job seekers under MGNREGS after the COVID-19 migrant crisis made it amply clear that this "surplus" labour force underwriting the urban economy, is living precarious lives. However, MGNREGS is inadequate to sustain livelihoods for the large number of rural citizens.

II. Building Livelihoods around Everyday Objects of Use

- There is a need to revive varied rural economies building around everyday objects that people use. The environmentally destructive industrial production systems, emissions laden supply chains and toxic plastic and other waste generated from discarding objects of everyday use need to be replaced with environmentally sustainable production and consumption systems.

- This would mean transforming our aspirations from mass consumption of cheap, standardised products to more equitable consumption of locally produced crafts, goods and services that would both, help local producers and artisans economically, and also promote ecologically sustainable consumption. [52]
- This would require reframing the understanding of 'quality' of produce in the minds of consumers. Standardised and uniform may not always imply 'good' quality because it may be possible to obtain it only through environmentally toxic industrial processes. Handmade products would necessarily be variable and non-uniform but they would potentially be more ecologically friendly.

III. Landless Workers

- There is a need to provide a living wage (not a minimum wage calculated using calorie intake) to all workers which would cover food, clothing and shelter for a family along with their educational, health and social needs.

IV. Role of Technology and Recovering the Dignity of Labour

- There would be role for technology in these processes, but one that would reduce the drudgery of labour without dispensing with the need for labour altogether, and recognising the role of physical labour in producing good health. [77]
- This would also necessitate recovering the dignity of labour from the shackles of the caste system.
- Policy efforts would need to a) broad-base artisanal skills through a process of institutionalisation of skill formation so as to undermine caste monopolies and b) ensure that such skills are continuously adapted to changing market and material conditions. In doing so, the unity of intellectual and manual labour that characterises craft/artisanal labour should be recognised.

V. Pastoralists

- The need is to support pastoralists and enable those who want to continue their traditional work by thinking about ways to link their produce with the market so that they can earn their livelihood, address the challenges in accessing foraging grounds, and legally recognize their right of movement and usage of resources over their traditional movement area. [54]

- Pastoralism continues to provide a valid livelihood for millions of people and has the potential to continue to do so. But the future of pastoralism depends on the ecological restoration and sustainable utilisation of rangelands, the improvement of livestock productivity and the resolution of resource conflicts in ways that facilitate the integration of pastoralism, agriculture and silviculture. [55]

VI. Women Farmers and Artisans

- The huge knowledge base of women in relation to genetic diversity, cultivation practices, storage, processing and cooking as well as their skills in craft and textiles must be recognised and supported. For instance, along with knowing which varieties are short duration or drought resistant, women's knowledge would invariably include, which ones cook faster, taste better, store longer, and are not attacked by pests.

- Technologies that are suitable for reducing the drudgery of women's labour must be promoted.

Why Produce and Consume Local?

I. Promote Local Procurement and Distribution

- Promote the decentralisation of institutional market activities i.e. encouraging local procurement and local distribution for PDS, mid-day meal, nutrition programs, and local processing of horticulture products etc. As opposed to providing incentives like MSP for only a select set of crops, this can *incentivise the production of a locally appropriate* (suitable to the local ecology and season) and *nutritious food basket.* It can also help in strengthening access to markets for farmers, especially small and marginal producers.

- Invest in the 23000 rural periodic haats (markets) and create regular markets and processing infrastructure at the village level itself, to enable *local processing and marketing at source.* This can help support the livelihoods of farmers by providing them access to markets locally (eschewing transportation costs) and also enhanced access to nutritious foods.

II. Reorient Marketing Strategy towards Domestic Demand

- Reorient our marketing strategy away from commodity chain value maximisation (i.e. linking the producers of specific crops to the processing and consumption value chain associated with it), which makes farmers grow monoculture crops for urban and export markets, thus, increasing the risk of, both, crop failure and price failure/collapse.

- Rather than being dependent on export markets for niche and exotic food items, it may be helpful to make policies that create and fulfill domestic demand for a nutritive and locally appropriate food basket.

- This would have to be linked to *providing viable livelihoods* to the broad swathe of rural citizens so that they can begin to afford locally produced foods and products.

- Producing and consuming locally or within a given region will *reduce the emissions accruing due to transportation* of products, including food, across long distances, thus, directly contribute towards climate change mitigation. It will also promote local food cultures and support the livelihoods of artisans and those in other allied rural occupations.

How Can Agricultural Marketing Be Made Accountable?

I. Reform the Mandi System

- Break local, regional and national oligopolies of traders / companies through the strong *implementation of competition laws* and by having more buyers (small and large traders, companies, cooperatives, Food Corporation of India) participating in the mandi auction.

- Make marketing institutions more *accountable to public officials and farmers* by opening their financial statements and working decisions to the scrutiny of elected public representatives and institutions like the gram sabha.

- Provide fair, accountable and easily accessible dispute raising and resolution mechanisms at each marketplace.

- *Improve market yard infrastructure* such as installing electronic weighbridges, electronic weighing scales, covered sheds, grading facilities for farmers, electronic price display, computerised record keeping etc.

- Become centres of distribution for all local food needs including government sponsored programs (PDS, mid-day meal, ICDS etc.), urban centres and private retail to support financial viability.

II. Farmer Producer Organisations

- Farmer producer organisations (FPOs, producer companies or PCs) have been considered as a means to increase the bargaining power of farmers by pooling together produce. However, they require extensive handholding and support to become viable and compete with private traders in the mandi or private agribusinesses that have much deeper pockets and far greater political power. So far, only a handful of these PCs have been able to become financially viable. Sahyadri Farms in Maharashtra with a membership of 8000 farmers and a turnover of Rs 300 crores is one such example. [35][101]

- There are a number of *challenges faced by FPOs* with respect to lack of easy and timely credit, burdensome regulatory compliances and taxation, logistics and infrastructure (lack of adequate storage facilities, systems for grading and sorting of produce), governance, human resources for planning and conducting business. [40]

- Some case studies of FPOs have demonstrated an increase in income of small and marginal farmers but lack of awareness and willingness amongst farmers to join FPOs as members is a problem.

- It is important that leadership and *decision making powers within FPOs are democratised and diversified* to include women farmers as well as farmers from underprivileged socio-economic backgrounds. [48]

Why Do Adivasi And Tribal Regions Require Special Attention?

I. Unjust Appropriation of Land and Resources

- India has nearly 100 million indigenous peoples, nearly 20% of the global indigenous population. The indigenous peoples of India are concentrated in some of the best forests and mineral rich lands. They have sustained not just forests but also treasure troves of biodiversity through sophisticated agroforestry practices.

- However the indigenous communities, especially of mainland India (Adivasis), have historically suffered *enormous injustice, violence and displacement by colonial and postcolonial regimes of extraction.* The liberalization of the economy since the 1980s intensified the unjust and undemocratic appropriation of these lands and resources by corporate sectors and state agencies.

- These regions have been *subject to intense violence* and this has led to the forced displacement of several lakhs of people. The 'Scheduled Tribes' (STs) constitute only 8.6 percent of Indian population, but at least *40% of the people displaced* or adversely affected by development projects between 1951 to 1990 are STs. [120][9] The Ministry of Tribal Affairs estimates the number of ST peoples displaced between 1951-1990 for dams, sanctuaries, etc. to be about 85 lakhs. [107] Of these, only 21 lakhs received some rehabilitation package. [107]

- Consequently, Adivasi peoples migrate across towns and cities, *working as informal labour* in workshops and at construction sites and in homes as domestic help.
- Scattered evidence suggests that the Adivasis and Dalits constituted a large section of the 'migrant workers' whose lives and livelihoods were devastated by the COVID-19 lockdown in March 2020. [121]

India has nearly **20%** of the world's indigenous population numbering almost **100 million.**

Scheduled Tribes comprise at least **40%** of the people displaced or adversely affected by development projects between 1951 to 1991.

II. Forest Rights Act (FRA)

- The Scheduled Tribes and Other Traditional Forest Dwellers (Recognition of Forest Rights) Act, 2006, was enacted to protect Adivasi groups and balance the right to environment with their right to life and livelihood. [33] The law recognises customary rights of people over forest land (up to 4 hectares) and gives them legal document of ownership of their traditional habitation. [32]
- However, since enactment of the law, out of 42.2 lakh applications which have been filed for the settlement of rights, 19.4 lakhs have been rejected. Only 54,591.07 sq km out of a total occupation area of 112,000 sq km of forest land has been recognised. There is a question mark over whether due process provided by the Act has been followed by gram sabhas and the States before the *claims of people have been rejected.* [32]

- While the ***FRA has been violated in practice***, there are other laws and policies such as the Compensatory Afforestation Fund Act 2016, Draft National Forest Policy 2018, Draft Indian Forest (Amendment) 2019 and the establishment of the District Mineral Foundations, which have strengthened the hands of the forest department / administration and the district bureaucracy at the expense of gram sabhas, to control the forest and its resources. These have severely eroded the rights of the tribal communities.

- As of June 2019, there were 56,000 crores available in the compensatory afforestation fund – indicating the scale of forest destruction. This, without accounting for large scale and rampant illegal mining, as documented by the Justice M.B. Shah Commission of Enquiry (2014). [21]

- The ***compensatory forests are often monoculture***, commercial plantations of eucalyptus etc., which cause further ecological damage and displacement of forest-dwellers / Adivasis. [108]

III. Valuing Indigenous and Experiential Knowledge for Sustainable Livelihoods and Conservation

- Forested areas must be seen as co-dwelling spaces where biodiverse flora and fauna have been nurtured and conserved by traditional forest-dwellers and Adivasis. Policies must enable Adivasis, indigenous and traditional forest-dwellers their rights to the forests, thus, safeguarding both their democratic rights and their ways and knowledge systems of conservation and food production.

- Promoting decentralised, localised systems and practices of biodiversity conservation along with assured rights and social protection to original forest dwellers will ensure more equitable and sustainable livelihoods and food security in these regions. [65]

What Can Be New Indices and Measurements for Evaluating Rural Economies?

I. DeGrowth

Prioritise social and ecological well-being through radical redistribution, reduction in the material size of the global economy, and a shift in common values towards care, solidarity and autonomy. Transforming societies to ensure environmental justice and a good life for all within planetary boundaries. [66]

II. Energy Balance Index

In this metric, sustainability in agriculture is defined as whether a farm household is able to generate an energy surplus given that all its living members including animals are in possession of sufficient calorie intake. It is calculated as a difference between the output and the input of energy in the agricultural production process and is measured in real terms, independent of prices. Situated at the intersection of ecology and economics, such an energy input-output index can capture depletion of the groundwater table or loss of soil fertility in terms of increase in input energy through increased fertilizer and irrigation usage. [43]

III. Ecosystem Services

Any contribution towards mitigating climate change, can be captured in an ecosystem services metric. This can include surplus energy production, carbon sequestration, reduced fossil fuel use (diesel machinery, industrial inputs), and can be positively remunerated, thus, providing funding to farmers to transition towards sustainable farming practices. [43]

IV. Water Audit by Districts

This would analyse the use of water for various purposes within a district for industrial, domestic, commercial, agricultural and other uses. Allocations can be revised according to water availability and a socially equitable and environmentally sound criteria of use.

V. Farm Assessment Index

Based on a systems approach, the FAI is an aggregation of several indices broadly classified under three dimensions: ecological, social and economic indices. A number of indicators are chosen based on the stock and flow diagram of a farming system as well as their measurability under each of these three dimensions. The indicator values which capture elements such as biodiversity, soil health, water use, risks, resilience, employment, food security, productivity, and land tenure etc. under their respective dimensions are then aggregated. By using a composite index such as the FAI, a scientific and comprehensive assessment of farming systems can be carried out which would yield a better characterization as compared to those indices based on only income growth or productivity for assessing agriculture. [44]

VI. Water Intensity Index

This index entails two interrelated aspects: first, mapping the water productivity of crops in different parts of the country and second, calculating the average water productivity value for individual crops. The data generated should inform policy decisions regarding cropping patterns, export of primary produce from the country as well as improvements required in cultivation techniques in different parts of the country. For instance, such an index shows that the export of water guzzling crops such as paddy and sugarcane is like exporting scarce groundwater and must be stopped. According to a NABARD report, the average physical water productivity for top paddy growing states such as Punjab, West Bengal, Assam, Telangana, Andhra Pradesh, Haryana is almost twice as much as the bottom ones such as Madhya Pradesh and Karnataka demonstrating a scope for improvement in the latter group. [10]

VII. Quality Indices for Soil and Water

Quality indices of soil and water across rural India need to be devised to evaluate the need for changing practices linked to the use of agrochemicals in farming and other allied sectors. These indices should be comprehensive in nature. For instance, in the case of soil, it should go beyond the Soil Health Card related chemical parameters to include biological and physical parameters as well and should incorporate the principle of three Ms: Organic Matter, Microbes and Moisture holding capacity of the soil. [62]

VIII. Biodiversity Index

It is the scale to measure the diversity of species within an agroecosystem. The need is to devise an easy to use tool so as to monitor and observe variations in biodiversity over a period of time. The index should be such that the data can be aggregated to be used by the policymakers at various levels including state and national levels. [79]

IX. Food Miles / Product Miles

This measures the environmental impact of food / products by measuring the distance travelled by it before reaching the consumer. Greater food / product miles entail a higher carbon footprint through transportation and industrialisation of agri-production. Lowering food miles would involve discouraging of long-distance sourcing and encouraging a dietary shift towards locally produced items. While this may not work for all items (some local items may be environmentally degrading, some items would need to come from long distances) it can act as an important indicator towards developing sustainable production and consumption systems. [47]

15 Conclusion: What Can Farmers and Others Do to Make the Rural Relevant?

The solutions for problems faced by rural India do not lie in the rural alone. *Urban residents will have to change their own consumption patterns* and expectations about what it means to live a 'good' life, else rural spaces will continue to get integrated adversely into exploitative systems. Government policies and corporate strategies need to be rethought from the perspective of climate change and ecological limits to growth. At the same time, the inherent inequalities of current levels of consumption need to be reconsidered and concrete steps taken to enable the marginalised majority to improve their well-being.

At the same time, only farmers and rural residents can best represent their own interests. They must engage with new ideas and alternatives instead of subscribing to old and dominant models that are to their disadvantage. Rural residents representing diverse occupations should assert their citizenship rights. Citizens must go beyond caste and religious associations and work in collaborative teams and networks. New and alternative ways to make the rural and agricultural a thriving/flourishing economy and society are possible. *Farmers and rural residents must lead the way through collective mobilisation* towards this goal.

We must *reclaim the "rural" as a positive space of transformation*, not as a residual, lacking or disadvantaged space. It is imperative to think of rural-rural linkages of production and consumption rather than a one way track of rural to urban or urban as the answer to the rural. This also entails a direct focus on the marginalised majority--underprivileged caste groups, adivasi groups, artisans, landless workers and most importantly, women.

The state and the market have both traversed problematic development trajectories in relation to rural India. Over-centralisation, a distorted subsidy regime, populist policies, over-emphasis on limited indices such as the GDP or productivity to the exclusion of others--these have all dogged the state. The market has been no answer with cartelisation, dangerous levels of control over inputs and markets by a select few private players and corporations, a patent regime favouring formal innovation systems and privatisation of knowledge, deregulation leading to excessive extraction and use of resources with complete disregard for dumping the waste of industrial processes.

However, the ***state can be held accountable*** for its actions and a collective demand for decentralisation and democratisation of rural and agricultural policies will go a long way in bringing the voices of the marginalised into policy making process and strengthen the democratic fabric of the nation. Working with state governments has already borne fruit in the last several years. While the centre may provide overarching guidelines, it is imperative that there is ***freedom to frame policies and guide agendas at the local level.*** This requires capacity building to enable economic, social, ecological and technical planning at the decentralised level (down to the gram panchayat).

The COVID-19 lockdown has shown the importance of the rural as the life-blood of the economy. The steady stream of walking migrants, women and men with children in tow, was living testament to the extractive, exploitative relations of the urban to the rural. Ironically, while formal indices consider agriculture to be contributing the least to the economy, it is the only sector showing vitality in the current phase, post-lockdown. Beyond the ecological implications, *redefining what is growth and well-being* is the way to come together to remake rural India into a livable, democratic, just, sustainable, and diverse place.

Sources

1. Gulati, Ashok, Marco A. Ferroni, Yuan Zhou, and Indian Council for Research on International Economic Relations, eds. 2018. *Supporting Indian Farms the Smart Way.* New Delhi: Academic Foundation.

2. Vaidyanathan, A. 2007. "Discussing 'Inclusive Growth' Ahead of its Time." *Economic and Political Weekly* 42 (30): 3096–3099.

3. Das, Keshab. 2011. "Rural industrialization in India: Enhancing reach and returns." in *Micro and small enterprises in India: The era of reforms* edited by Keshab Das. New Delhi: Routledge.

4. Shiao, Tien, Andrew Maddocks, Chris Carson, and Emma Loizeaux. 2015. "3 Maps Explain India's Growing Water Risks." World Resources Institute. February 26, 2015. https://www.wri.org/blog/2015/02/3-maps-explain-india-s-growing-water-risks.

5. "India Watertool." n.d. https://www.indiawatertool.in

6. *Economic Survey 2015-16.* 2016. Ministry of Finance, Government of India. https://www.indiabudget.gov.in/budget2016-2017/survey.asp

7. Himanshu. 2015. "India's Flawed Fertilizer Policy." *Livemint,* April 1, 2015. https://www.livemint.com/Opinion/XCCJwEzbzwiyWFYfK1wRdO/Indias-flawed-fertilizer-policy.html.

8. Raina, Rajeswari S., and Debanjana Dey. 2016. "The Valuation Conundrum: Biodiversity and Science-Policy Interface in India's Livestock Sector." *Economic and Political Weekly* 51(47): 70-78.

9. Wahi, Namita, Ankit Bhatia. 2018. *The Legal Regime and Political Economy of Land Rights of Scheduled Tribes in the Scheduled Areas of India*, Centre for Policy Research, New Delhi, 2018.

10. Sharma, Bharat R., Ashok Gulati, Gayathri Mohan, Stuti Manchanda, Indro Ray, and Upali Amarasinghe. 2018. *Water Productivity Mapping Of Major Indian Crops*. NABARD and ICRIER. https://www.nabard.org/auth/writereaddata/tender/1806181128Water%20Productivity%20Mapping%20o f%20Major%20Indian%20Crops,%20Web%20Version%20(Low%20Resolution%20PDF).pdf.

11. Otte, J., D. Roland-Holst, D. Pfeiffer, R. Soares-Magalhaes, J. Rushton, J. Graham, and E. Silbergeld. 2007. *Industrial Livestock Production and Global Health Risks*. Research Report. Pro-Poor Livestock Policy Initiative. http://www.fao.org/3/a-bp285e.pdf.

12. FAO, IFAD, UNICEF, WFP and WHO. 2019. *The State of Food Security and Nutrition in the World 2019. Safeguarding against economic slowdowns and downturns.* FAO. http://www.fao.org/3/ca5162en/ca5162en.pdf

13. Vaidyanathan, A. 2010. *Agricultural Growth in India: Role of Technology, Incentives, and Institutions.* Oxford Collected Essays. New Delhi: Oxford University Press.

14. Raina, Rajeswari S. 2012. "Agriculture in the Environment: Are Sustainable Climate Friendly Systems Possible in India?" in *Handbook of Climate Change and India* ed. Navroz K. Dubash. Abingdon, Oxon ; N.Y: Earthscan.

15. "India." n.d. Research Program on Climate Change, Agriculture and Food Security. Accessed June 13, 2020. https://ccafs.cgiar.org/india#.XxlbPS0w1QI.

16. Shukla, Arvind K., Pankaj K. Tiwari, and Chandra Prakash. 2014. "Micronutrients Deficiencies Vis-a-Vis Food and Nutritional Security of India." *Indian Journal of Fertilisers* 10 (12): 94–112.

17. Kranthi, K. R., and Glenn Davis Stone. 2020. "Long-Term Impacts of Bt Cotton in India." *Nature Plants* 6 (3): 188–96. https://doi.org/10.1038/s41477-020-0615-5.

18. Staff, DTE. 2018. "Uttarakhand Cloudburst: Urbanisation, Warming Continue to Intensify the Impact." *DownToEarth (DTE)*, July 3, 2018. https://www.downtoearth.org.in/news/natural-disasters/uttarakhand-cloudburst-urbanisation-warming-co ntinue-to-intensify-the-impact-60999.

19. Padmanabhan, Vishnu, Sneha Alexander, and Prachi Srivastava. 2019. "The Growing Threat of Climate Change in India." *Livemint*, July 21, 2019. https://www.livemint.com/news/india/the-growing-threat-of-climate-change-in-india-1563716968468.html.

20. Eliazer Nelson, Ann Raeboline Lincy, Kavitha Ravichandran, and Usha Antony. 2019. "The Impact of the Green Revolution on Indigenous Crops of India." *Journal of Ethnic Foods* 6 (1): 8. https://doi.org/10.1186/s42779-019-0011-9.

21. "Shah Commission of Enquiry." n.d. Ministry of Mines, Government of India. Accessed September 26, 2020. https://www.mines.gov.in/ViewData/index?mid=1333.

22. DeFries, Ruth, Ashwini Chhatre, Kyle Frankel Davis, Arnab Dutta, Jessica Fanzo, Suparna Ghosh-Jerath, Samuel Myers, Narasimha D. Rao, and Matthew R. Smith. 2018. "Impact of Historical Changes in Coarse Cereals Consumption in

India on Micronutrient Intake and Anemia Prevalence." *Food and Nutrition Bulletin* 39 (3): 377–92. https://doi.org/10.1177/0379572118783492.

23. "India at a Glance." n.d. FAO in India. Accessed June 25, 2020. http://www.fao.org/india/fao-in-india/india-at-a-glance/en/.

24. Khanna, Ruchika M. 2020. "Long Road Ahead on the Farm Front." *The Tribune*, April 6, 2020. https://www.tribuneindia.com/news/features/long-road-ahead-on-the-farm-front-66390.

25. Compiled from Agricultural Wages Reports 2010-11 to 2017-18. Directorate of Economics and Statistics, Department Of Agriculture, Cooperation & Farmers Welfare, Ministry Of Agriculture & Farmers Welfare, Government of India. Accessed August 26, 2020. https://eands.dacnet.nic.in/AWIS.htm.

26. *Strengthening the Institutions, Infrastructure and Markets That Govern Agricultural Growth.* 2018. XIII. Structural Reforms and Governance Framework. Committee on Doubling Farmers' Income, Department of Agriculture, Cooperation and Farmers' Welfare, Ministry of Agriculture & Farmers' Welfare. http://farmer.gov.in/imagedefault/DFI/DFI%20Volume%2013.pdf.

27. *Agriculture Census 2015-16: All India Report on Number and Area of Operational Holdings.* 2019. Agriculture Census Division, Department of Agriculture, Co-operation & Farmers Welfare, Ministry of Agriculture & Farmers Welfare, Government of India. http://agcensus.nic.in/document/agcen1516/T1_ac_2015_16.pdf.

28. Varma, Subodh. 2018. "Caste Stranglehold in Agriculture." *Newsclick*, October 10, 2018. https://www.newsclick.in/caste-stranglehold-agriculture.

29. Vissa, Kiran. 2019. "Policy Meets Reality at District-Level: The Experiences of Kisan Mitra Helpline." In *Beyond Productivity and Populism: Reimagining India's Agricultural and Rural Policies*. Delhi. Compiled and Presented at the 2nd Network of Rural and Agrarian Studies (NRAS) Policy Conference.

30. Vasavi, A.R. 2009. "Suicides and the Making of India's Agrarian Distress." *South African Review of Sociology* 40 (1): 94–108. https://doi.org/10.1080/21528586.2009.10425102.

31. Agrawal, Nikhit Kumar. 2020. "Some Key Questions that Need to Be Answered About the Three Agricultural Ordinances." *The Wire*, June 24, 2020. https://thewire.in/agriculture/agriculture-ordinances-key-questions

32. Kukreti, Ishan, and Priya Ranjan Sahu. 2019. "Forest Rights Act: Who Is the Encroacher and Who Is Encroached Upon." *DownToEarth*, March 19, 2019. https://www.downtoearth.org.in/coverage/forests/forest-rights-act-who-is-the-encroacher-and-who-is- encroached-upon-63585.

33. Rajagopal, Krishnadas. 2019. "What Is Forest Rights Act?" *The Hindu*, March 2, 2019. https://www.thehindu.com/sci-tech/energy-and-environment/what-is-forest-rights-act/article26419298 .ece.

34. "Science for Doubling Farmers' Income." 2018. XII. Focusing Scientific Development and Technological Applications on Doubling Farmers' Income. Committee on Doubling Farmers' Income, Department of Agriculture, Cooperation and Farmers' Welfare, Ministry of Agriculture & Farmers' Welfare. http://farmer.gov.in/imagedefault/DFI/DFI%20Vol-12A.pdf.

35. Bhosale, Jayashree. 2018. "How Farmer Producer Company Model Can Transform Indian Agriculture," September 29, 2018. https://economictimes.indiatimes.com/news/economy/agriculture/how-farmer-producer-company-mo

del-can-transform-indian-agriculture/articleshow/66000269. cms?from=mdr.

36. *Status Of Marketing Infrastructure Under Electronic National Agriculture Markets: A Quick Study.* 2018. Mumbai: National Bank for Agriculture and Rural Development, Department of Economic Analysis and Research. https://www.nabard.org/auth/writereaddata/tender/0904195131Status%20of%20Marketing%20Infrast ructure%20under%20Electronic%20National%20Agriculture%20Market_A%20Quick%20Study. pdf.

37. "Corporate Concentration in Agriculture and Food." 2020. Focus on the Global South, Alternative Law Forum and Rosa Luxemburg Stiftung. https://focusweb.org/wp-content/uploads/2020/07/CorpConAg_Dossier_FocusJuly2020-1. pdf.

38. Thakur, J., B. Rao, Arvind Rajwanshi, H. Parwana, and Rajesh Kumar. 2008. "Epidemiological Study of High Cancer among Rural Agricultural Community of Punjab in Northern India." *International Journal of Environmental Research and Public Health* 5 (5): 399–407. https://doi.org/10.3390/ijerph5050399.

39. Chatterjee, Shoumitro, and Mekhala Krishnamurthy. 2020. "Understanding and Misunderstanding E-NAM." *Seminar,* January 2020. https://www.india-seminar. com/2020/725/725_shoumitro_and_mekhala.htm.

40. "Framing Futures: National Conference on Farmer Producer Organizations." 2017. Workshop. Gujarat: Dr. Verghese Kurien Centre of Excellence Institute of Rural Management Anand. https://irma.ac.in/pdf/randp/2046_98300.pdf.

41. "March of Agriculture since Independence and Growth Trends." 2018. XII. Historical Analysis and Examination of India's Agricultural Production and Farmers' Income. Committee

on Doubling Farmers' Income, Department of Agriculture, Cooperation and Farmers' Welfare, Ministry of Agriculture & Farmers' Welfare. http://agricoop.gov.in/sites/default/files/DFI%20Volume%201.pdf.

42. Raina, Rajeswari S. 2019. "Agricultural sciences, technology and administration - centralisation and consolidation as a policy process problem." In *Beyond Productivity and Populism: Reimagining India's Agricultural and Rural Policies*. Delhi. Compiled and Presented at the 2nd Network of Rural and Agrarian Studies (NRAS) Policy Conference.

43. Nawn, Nandan. 2016. "Sustainability, Surplus and Survival: energetic explorations over agriculture." In *Economic Challenges for the Contemporary World: Essays in Honour of Prabhat Patnaik*, edited by M Das, S Kar and N Nawn. New Delhi: Sage

44. Muthuprakash, Siva, and Om Damani. 2019. "Developing Alternate Metrics of Success-Composite Indices Approach." In *Beyond Productivity and Populism: Reimagining India's Agricultural and Rural Policies*. Delhi. Compiled and Presented at the 2nd Network of Rural and Agrarian Studies (NRAS) Policy Conference.

45. Bag, Dinabandhu. 2000. "Pesticides and health risks." *Economic and Political Weekly* 35(38): 3381-3383.

46. Bathla, Seema, Sukhadeo Thorat, P K Joshi, and Bingxin Yu. 2017. "Where to Invest to Accelerate Agricultural Growth and Poverty Reduction." *Economic and Political Weekly* 52 (29): 36–45.

47. Iles, Alastair. 2005. "Learning in Sustainable Agriculture: Food Miles and Missing Objects."

48. *Environmental Values* 14 (2): 163–83. https://doi.org/10.3197/0963271054084894.

49. Prasad, C. Shambu, and Gautam Prateek. 2019. "Farming Futures: An Annotated Bibliography On Farmer Producer Organisations In India." Working Paper. Institute of Rural Management Anand, Gujarat. https://www.irma.ac.in/uploads/randp/pdf/2162_27777.pdf.

50. Sanyal, Kalyan, and Rajesh Bhattacharyya. 2009. "Beyond the Factory: Globalisation, Informalisation of Production and the New Locations of Labour." *Economic and Political Weekly* 44 (22).

51. NAAS. 2010. *Degraded and Wastelands of India: Status and Spatial Distribution*. National Academy of Agricultural Sciences, New Delhi.

52. "Working Group Report on Handicrafts for 12th Five Year Plan." n.d. Ministry of Textiles, Government of India. https://niti.gov.in/planningcommission.gov.in/docs/aboutus/committee/wrkgrp12/wg_handi1101.pdf

53. Banerjee, Madhulika. 2019. "Rural Artisans in the Contemporary:Policy and Politics of Sustainability." In *Beyond Productivity and Populism: Reimagining India's Agricultural and Rural Policies*. Delhi. Compiled and Presented at the 2nd Network of Rural and Agrarian Studies (NRAS) Policy Conference.

54. Donthi, Narasimha Reddy. 2019. "Undermining Rural Economy: Case of Handloom Sector." In *Beyond Productivity and Populism: Reimagining India's Agricultural and Rural Policies*. Delhi. Compiled and Presented at the 2nd Network of Rural and Agrarian Studies (NRAS) Policy Conference.

55. Saberwal, Vasant. 2019. "Pastoralism at the Cross-roads: The Need for and Outline of a Policy Framework." In *Beyond Productivity and Populism: Reimagining India's Agricultural and Rural Policies*. Delhi. Compiled and Presented at the 2nd

Network of Rural and Agrarian Studies (NRAS) Policy Conference.

56. *DownToEarth.* n.d. "Pastoralists at the Crossroads." Accessed June 25, 2020. https://www.downtoearth.org.in/indepth/pastoralists-at-the-crossroads-31823.

57. Horwith, B. 1985. "A role for intercropping in modern agriculture." *BioScience* 35(5): 286-291.

58. NRAS Collective. 2019. Concept Note for the Second Policy Conference of the Network of Rural and Agrarian Studies (NRAS) titled *Beyond Productivity and Populism: Reimagining India's Agricultural and Rural Policies.* Delhi.

59. NRAS Collective. 2019. Summary Report for the Second Policy Conference of the Network of Rural and Agrarian Studies (NRAS) titled *Beyond Productivity and Populism: Reimagining India's Agricultural and Rural Policies.* Delhi.

60. Dhaliwal, G.S., Vikas Jindal, and Bharathi Mohindru. 2015. "Crop Losses Due to Insect Pests: Global and Indian Scenario." *Indian Journal of Entomology* 77 (2): 165. https://doi.org/10.5958/0974-8172.2015.00033.4.

61. Krishnaiah, K., and N. R. G. Varma. 2012. "Changing insect pest scenario in the rice ecosystem—A national perspective." *Directorate of Rice Research Rajendranagar, Hyderabad, 2012,* 2-8. http://www.rkmp.co.in/sites/default/files/ris/research-themes/Changing%20Insect%20Pest%20Scena rio%20in%20 the%20Rice%20Ecosystem.pdf

62. Kranthi, K.R. 2015. "Whitefly –The Black Story." *Cotton Statistics & News,* 2015. http://cicr.org.in/pdf/Kranthi_art/Whitefly.pdf.

63. DST Centre for Policy Research IIT Delhi and others. 2017. Summary Report for the National Conference titled *India's*

Soils: Science-Policy-Practice Interfaces for Sustainable Futures . Delhi.

64. Rao, C. H. Hanumantha, and Ashok Gulati, Ashok. 1994. 'Indian Agriculture: Emerging Perspectives and Policy Issues." *Economic and Political Weekly*, 29(53): A158-A169.

65. Barker, Randolph, Robert W. Herdt, Beth Rose, and Beth Rose. 1985. *The Rice Economy of Asia.* Washington, D.C.: [Baltimore, Md.]: Resources for the Future; Distributed by Johns Hopkins University Press.

66. Sinha, Bishwajit, and Kallol Bhattacharyya. 2015. "Arsenic Toxicity in Rice with Special Reference to Speciation in Indian Grain and Its Implication on Human Health." *Journal of the Science of Food and Agriculture* 95 (7): 1435–44. https://doi.org/10.1002/jsfa.6839.

67. "What Is Degrowth?" n.d. Degrowth. Accessed September 26, 2020. https://www.degrowth.info/en/what-is-degrowth.

68. Nellemann, Christian, Monika MacDevette, Ton Manders, Bas Eickhout, Birger Svihus, Anne Gerdien Prins, and Bjorn P. Kaltenborn. eds. 2009. *The Environmental Food Crisis. The environment's role in averting future food crises: A UNEP rapid response assessment.* Arendal, Norway: UNEP.

69. "Minutes of 361st Special Meeting of Registration Committee (RC)." 2015. http://ppqs.gov.in/sites/default/files/361rc2015.pdf. "VDSA ICRISAT Database." n.d. http://vdsa.icrisat.ac.in/vdsa-database.aspx.

70. Vijayshankar, P.S. 2019. "Tribal Agriculture in Central India: Context and Challenges." In *Beyond Productivity and Populism: Reimagining India's Agricultural and Rural Policies.* Delhi. Compiled and Presented at the 2nd Network of Rural and Agrarian Studies (NRAS) Policy Conference.

71. "Economic Survey 2016-17." 2017. Ministry of Finance, Government of India. https://www.indiabudget.gov.in/budget2017-2018/survey.asp

72. "Economic Survey 2019-20." 2020. Ministry of Finance, Government of India. https://www.indiabudget.gov.in/economicsurvey/

73. Aga, Aniket. 2019. "Framing the problem of agrichemicals management as if the agrarian crisis mattered." In *Beyond Productivity and Populism: Reimagining India's Agricultural and Rural Policies*. Delhi. Compiled and Presented at the 2nd Network of Rural and Agrarian Studies (NRAS) Policy Conference.

74. Singh, Sukhpal. 2000. "Crisis in Punjab Agriculture." *Economic and Political Weekly* 35(23): 1889-1892. http://www.jstor.org/stable/4409349

75. Kumar, Richa. 2016. *Rethinking Revolutions: Soyabean, Choupals, and the Changing Countryside in Central India*. New Delhi, India: Oxford University Press.

76. Kumar, Richa. 2019. "India's Green Revolution and Beyond: Visioning Agrarian Futures on Selective Readings of Agrarian Pasts." *Economic and Political Weekly* 54(34): 41-48.

77. Tyagi, Bharat Bhushan, and Richa Kumar. 2020. "The Future of Farming: To What End and For What Purpose?" *Science, Technology and Society* 25(2): 256–72. https://doi.org/10.1177/0971721820902966.

78. Vasavi, A. R. 2012. *Shadow Space: Suicides and the Predicament of Rural India*. 1st ed. Gurgaon: Three Essays Collective.

79. Ahlawat, S.P., and S. Nivedhitha. n.d. "Agrobiodiversity Index: Role in Germplasm Collection and Conservation." Division of Plant Exploration and Germplasm Collection, ICAR-NBPGR.

http://www.nbpgr.ernet.in/Training_Management_PGR/ Compendium/10_Agrobiodiversity_Index_SP _Ahlawat.pdf.

80. Bhutani, Shalini. 2019. "National and Transnational Regimes in Innovation and the experience with intellectual property rights(IPRs)." In *Beyond Productivity and Populism: Reimagining India's Agricultural and Rural Policies*. Delhi. Compiled and Presented at the 2nd Network of Rural and Agrarian Studies (NRAS) Policy Conference.

81. "Unemployment Rate in India, CMIE." n.d. Accessed August 25, 2020. https://unemploymentinindia.cmie.com/kommon/ bin/sr.php?kall=wshowtab&tabno=0001.

82. "Status of Farmers' Income: Strategies for Accelerated Growth." 2018. XII. Inter-linkages between Input Costs, Diversification, Capital Formation and Income. Committee on Doubling Farmers' Income, Department of Agriculture, Cooperation and Farmers' Welfare, Ministry of Agriculture & Farmers' Welfare. http://farmer.gov.in/imagedefault/DFI/DFI%20 Volume%202.pdf.

83. "Annual Report: Periodic Labour Force Survey (PLFS) July 2017- June 2018." 2019. Annual Report. New Delhi: National Statistical Office, Ministry of Statistics and Programme Implementation. http://www.mospi.gov.in/sites/default/files/ publication_reports/Annual%20Report%2C%20PLFS%202 017-18_31052019.pdf.

84. Pattnaik, Itishree, Kuntala Lahiri-Dutt, Stewart Lockie, and Bill Pritchard. 2018. "The Feminization of Agriculture or the Feminization of Agrarian Distress? Tracking the Trajectory of Women in Agriculture in India." *Journal of the Asia Pacific Economy* 23 (1): 138–55. https://doi.org/10.1080/13547860 .2017.1394569.

85. Mohan, Tarini. 2017. "A field of her own." *The Indian Express*, August 4, 2017. https://indianexpress.com/article/opinion/

columns/indian-women-farmers-agriculture-sector-patriarch
y-land-ownership-4781311/

86. Anugula, Himakiran. 2019. "Conserving Natural Resources, Mainstreaming Agrobiodiversity and Addressing Climate Change: Livestock." In *Beyond Productivity and Populism: Reimagining India's Agricultural and Rural Policies*. Delhi. Compiled and Presented at the 2nd Network of Rural and Agrarian Studies (NRAS) Policy Conference.

87. Patra, Suman, Satiprasad Sahoo, Pulak Mishra, and Subhash Chandra Mahapatra. 2018. "Impacts of Urbanization on Land Use /Cover Changes and Its Probable Implications on Local Climate and Groundwater Level." *Journal of Urban Management* 7 (2): 70–84. https://doi.org/10.1016/j.jum.2018.04.006.

88. Mazoomdaar, Jay. 2020. "Explained: Reading the new State of Forest Report 2019." *The Indian Express*, January 7, 2020. https:// indianexpress.com/article/explained/reading-the-new-forest-survey-of-india-report-prakash-jav adekar-6201259 /

89. Sriram, M.S. 2019. "Re-Territorialising the Landscape: Techno-financial Regimes of Land, Insurance, Credit and Debt." In *Beyond Productivity and Populism: Reimagining India's Agricultural and Rural Policies*. Delhi. Compiled and Presented at the 2nd Network of Rural and Agrarian Studies (NRAS) Policy Conference.

90. Singh, Parminder Jeet. 2019. "Datafication of agriculture in the digital age." In *Beyond Productivity and Populism: Reimagining India's Agricultural and Rural Policies*. Delhi. Compiled and Presented at the 2nd Network of Rural and Agrarian Studies (NRAS) Policy Conference.

91. Sen, Amartya. 1981. *Poverty and Famines: An Essay on Entitlement and Deprivation*. Oxford: New York: Clarendon Press; Oxford University Press.

92. Vandermeer, John, Aniket Aga, Jake Allgeier, Catherine Badgley, Regina Baucom, Jennifer Blesh, Lilly F. Shapiro, et al. 2018. "Feeding Prometheus: An Interdisciplinary Approach for Solving the Global Food Crisis." *Frontiers in Sustainable Food Systems* 2: 39. https://doi.org/10.3389/fsufs.2018.00039.

93. Tomlinson, Isobel. 2013. "Doubling Food Production to Feed the 9 Billion: A Critical Perspective on a Key Discourse of Food Security in the UK." *Journal of Rural Studies* 29 (January): 81–90. https://doi.org/10.1016/j.jrurstud.2011.09.001.

94. Sabarmatee. 2019. "Does Patch work really work for farming and farmers? Decentralising processes for planning, implementation and co-creation of knowledge at village level." In *Beyond Productivity and Populism: Reimagining India's Agricultural and Rural Policies*. Delhi. Compiled and Presented at the 2nd Network of Rural and Agrarian Studies (NRAS) Policy Conference.

95. "Agricultural Wages in India 2017-18." n.d. Directorate of Economics and Statistics, Department Of Agriculture, Cooperation & Farmers Welfare, Ministry Of Agriculture & Farmers Welfare, Government of India. Accessed August 26, 2020. https://eands.dacnet.nic.in/AgriWages2017-18.pdf.

96. FAO, and Commission on Genetic Resources for Food and Agriculture. 2019. *The State of the World's Biodiversity for Food and Agriculture*.

97. Kalamkar, S.S. 2009. "Urbanisation and Agricultural Growth in India." *Indian Journal of Agricultural Economics* 64(3): 442–61.

98. Government of India. 2017. "Pocket Book of Agricultural Statistics." Ministry of Agriculture & Farmers Welfare. http://agricoop.nic.in/sites/default/files/pocketbook_0.pdf.

99.   The Wire Staff. 2019. "After 3-Year Delay, Government Releases Farmer Suicide Data." *The Wire*, October 8, 2019. https://thewire.in/agriculture/farmer-suicides-data.

100. Tiwary, Deeptiman. 2020. "Steady Decline in Farm Sector Suicides from 2016 to 2019, NCRB Data Shows." *The Indian Express*, September 3, 2020. https://indianexpress.com/article/india/steady-decline-in-farm-sector-suicides-from-2016-to-2019-ncr b-data-shows-6580833/.

101. Prasad, C. Shambu. 2019. "Farming As An Enterprise - Ten Years of FPO Movement in India." State of India's Livelihoods Report 2019. https://www.livelihoods-india.org/uploads-livelihoodsasia/subsection_data/state-of-indias-livelihoods-r eport-2019.pdf.

102. Deb, Debal. 2017. "Folk Rice Varieties, Traditional Knowledge and Nutritional Security in South Asia." In *Agroecology, Ecosystems, and Sustainability in the Tropics*. Studera Press. http://www.studerapress.com/product/agroecology-ecosystems-and-sustainability-in-the-tropics/.

103. "Ministry of Textiles, Government of India." n.d. Development Commissioner (Handicrafts). Accessed September 23, 2020. http://www.handicrafts.nic.in/Page.aspx?MID=BOII5FUynjpl5RZJJ8nW1g==#.

104. "The Fertiliser Association of India." n.d. Accessed September 24, 2020. https://www.faidelhi.org/general/con-npk.pdf.

105. Tiwari, V. M., J. Wahr, and S. Swenson. 2009. "Dwindling Groundwater Resources in Northern India, from Satellite Gravity Observations." *Geophysical Research Letters* 36 (18): L18401. https://doi.org/10.1029/2009GL039401.

106. Rodell, Matthew, Isabella Velicogna, and James S. Famiglietti. 2009. "Satellite-Based Estimates of Groundwater Depletion

in India." *Nature* 460 (7258): 999–1002. https://doi.org/10.1038/nature08238.

107. "Annual Report 2015-16." n.d. Ministry of Tribal Affairs, Government of India. https://tribal.nic.in/writereaddata/AnnualReport/AnnualReport2015-16.pdf.

108. Choudhury, Chitrangada. 2019. "A Rs 56,000-Cr 'Afforestation' Fund Threatens India's Indigenous Communities." *IndiaSpend*, June 25, 2019. https://www.indiaspend.com/a-rs-56000-cr-afforestation-fund-threatens-indias-indigenous-communities/.

109. CGWB. 2019. "Dynamic Groundwater Resources of India 2017." Central Groundwater Board, Delhi.

110. CPCB. 2018. "River Stretches for Restoration of Water Quality (Statewise and Prioritywise)." Central Pollution Control Board, Government of India.

111. NSSO. 2015. "Some Characteristics of Agricultural Households, NSSO 70th Round, Report No. 569(70/33/1)." National Sample Survey Organisation, New Delhi.

112. NABARD. 2019. "NABARD Financial Inclusion Survey (NAFIS) 2017." National Bank of Agriculture and Rural Development, Mumbai.

113. Krishnaji, N. 2018. "Dynamics of Land Inequality: Polarization or Pauperization?." *Indian Journal of Human Development* 12(2): 1–13.

114. MoES. 2019. "Assessment of Climate Change over the Indian Region: A Report of the Ministry of Earth Sciences (MoES)." Government of India.

115. "State Wise Macro Nutrient Status for Cycle -II." n.d. Macro Nutrients Status - State Wise. Accessed September 26, 2020. https://soilhealth.dac.gov.in/PublicReports/MacroNutrientsStateWiseNPK.

116. Dhaliwal, G.S., Vikas Jindal, and A.K. Dhawan. 2010. "Insect Pest Problems and Crop Losses: Changing Trends." *Indian Journal of Ecology* 37 (1): 1–7.

117. Choudhury, Chitrangada. 2014. "The Barefoot Conservator." *People's Archive of Rural India,* December 16, 2014. https://ruralindiaonline.org/articles/the-barefoot-conservator-debal-deb/.

118. "Crafting a Livelihood: Building Sustainability for Indian Artisans." 2013. Dasra. https://www.dasra.org/assets/uploads/resources/Crafting%20a%20Livelihood%20-%20Building%20S ustainability%20for%20Indian%20Artisans.pdf.

119. Dastidar, Avishek G. 2020. "1.06 Cr Migrants Returned from Cities to Home States during Lockdown: Govt." *The Indian Express,* September 23, 2020. https://indianexpress.com/article/india/1-06-cr-migrants-returned-from-cities-to-home-states-during-lo ckdown-govt-6606918/.

120. Fernandes, Walter. 2008. "Sixty Years of Development induced Displacement in India: Scale, Impacts and the Search for Alternatives." in *India Social Development Report 2008: Development and Displacement* ed. Hari Mohan Mathur. Council for Social Development. New Delhi: Oxford University Press. http://csdindia.org/publications/social-development-report/2008-social-development-report/.

121. Choudhury, Chitrangada, and Aniket Aga. 2020. "India's Pandemic Response Is A Caste Atrocity." *NDTV,* May 27, 2020. https://www.ndtv.com/opinion/india-s-pandemic-response-is-a-caste-atrocity-2236094.